I0884498

# Meet the Parents

*Meet the Parents* is an essential guide for school leaders and classroom teachers looking to build stronger and more productive relationships with the families of pupils. This book uses more than 40 years of experience to explain techniques for uniting families with a range of backgrounds and a variety of circumstances, and highlights the most successful approaches for encouraging and developing the home-school partnership. Drawing on case studies and real-life examples, Lepkowska and Nightingale unpick the reasons behind barriers to learning and examine the issues that cause parents to be demotivated from engaging with schools.

The authors cover a range of important topics, from the long-standing concerns to modern problems, including:

- Making the most of parents' evening.
- Special Educational Needs and Disability.
- Bereavement, divorce and loss.
- Raising the aspirations of parents and children.
- Influence of the media and online safety.

*Meet the Parents* aims to aid head teachers, senior leaders, classroom practitioners and student teachers – and any other school staff who wish to develop a more effective ongoing home-school partnership. Recognising the vital need for parental engagement with children's learning, this book will help schools and families to come together and provide the best support possible for every child.

**Dorothy Lepkowska** is an award-winning journalist, who has written about education for a number of national and specialist publications, as well as for leading educational organisations, for the past 27 years, and more recently about parenting. She is married and has a child in primary school.

**Julie Nightingale** is a freelance journalist and has written for the national and specialist media for more than 25 years. She also leads the MA Magazine Journalism course at Nottingham Trent University.

# Meet the Parents

## How Schools Can Work Effectively with Families to Support Children's Learning

Dorothy Lepkowska
and Julie Nightingale

Routledge
Taylor & Francis Group
LONDON AND NEW YORK

First edition published 2019
by Routledge
2 Park Square, Milton Park, Abingdon, Oxon, OX14 4RN

and by Routledge
52 Vanderbilt Avenue, New York, NY 10017

*Routledge is an imprint of the Taylor & Francis Group, an informa business*



*British Library Cataloguing-in-Publication Data*
A catalogue record for this book is available from the British Library

*Library of Congress Cataloging-in-Publication Data*
A catalog record for this book has been requested

ISBN: 978-1-138-48945-5 (hbk)
ISBN: 978-1-138-48946-2 (pbk)
ISBN: 978-1-351-03754-9 (ebk)

Typeset in Galliard
by Apex CoVantage, LLC

# Contents

# Acknowledgements

## Dorothy's acknowledgements

Thanks to all the schools who made time for me to visit and hear their stories. Their candour in recounting their experiences was as inspirational as some of their methods: Yvonne Hewson and Karen Ward, Bure Park Primary School; Bronwen Hywel, John Perryn Primary School; David Taylor, Stanley Park High School; Ed Vainker and Kay Stone, The Reach Academy. And to those who made time for prolonged telephone conversations: Andy Grace, Boulevard Academy; Harinder Kaur, The Co-op Academy in Leeds; Gareth Morewood, Priestnall School; Stephen Wilkinson, Canford School; Leo Winkley, St Peter's School.

The voices of parents in this book are crucial to understanding the tensions and conflicts that often exist between the school and home and I am grateful to Debby Elly, Barbara Kenny, Emilie-Kate Kidd, Eileen Prior and Caroline Stewart and her son Ben for sharing their thoughts and experiences.

My thanks also go to the consultants and organisations who work to support schools, and parents, in the education and development of children and young people and who added context and insights into some of the issues discussed: Kay Joel, NSPCC; Mark Lehain, New Schools Network; Anul Manota, Karma Nirvana; Lorraine Petersen, Lorraine Petersen Educational Consultancy.

And last, but not least, my thanks to the learned academics and experts working in universities who shared their research, articles and perspectives: Dr Janet Goodall, University of Bath; Dimitra Hartas, Associate Professor, University of Warwick; Dr Ruth Hewston, University of Worcester; Sarah Owens; Dr Martyn Walker, University of Huddersfield.

## Julie's acknowledgements

Thanks to all of the teachers, support staff, heads and other leaders, academics and fellow journalists who gave up their time to help with this book. People have been incredibly generous with their time and their insights, frequently leading to whole new lines of enquiry, and writing this book has been a great learning experience for me as a result.

For the digital safety chapter, I'd like to thank Mark Bridges, Writhlington School; Daniel Everest, King's Ely; Steve Farmer; Will Gardner of ChildNet; Traci Good; and James Summerson of the White Horse Federation. David Wright, director of the UK Safer Internet Centre, has helped me with numerous stories on this important topic over many years now and I am indebted to him for his patience in explaining some of the complexities and for his expertise.

Katie Koehler of Child Bereavement UK, Elaine Roub and Alison Thomas of Cruse, Jo Laker of Braithwaite Primary and Sally Paul all offered invaluable help in researching the important but often overlooked area of how schools and communities deal with bereavement. Particular thanks go to 'Jess and Paula' who were willing to share their experience as a bereaved family in the hope that it would benefit others.

Chris Wheatley of the Flying High Trust, Phil Denton of St Bede's Catholic High School and Louise Payne of St Edmund Arrowsmith RC High School helped explore the complex topic of raising aspiration for children and communities. Thanks here, too, to Nasser Latif and Laura Bates of Nottingham Trent University and Sharon Mullen at Nottingham City Council.

Finally, thanks to fellow journalists, writers, editors and comms people, Nick Bannister, John Holt, Tracy Powell, Dan Russell, Stephanie Sparrow and Sophie Turner and to school leaders Vic Goddard of Passmores and John Dexter, now with Nottingham City Council.

# 1 Introduction

*Meet the Parents* was inspired by our combined 40-plus years of working in education journalism, during which we have interviewed and met hundreds of heads, teachers and governors – and, indeed, parents. A recurring theme in those conversations in more recent years was the challenges schools face in finding ways to engage parents in order to support children's learning and well-being.

While we use the term 'parents' throughout the book, we include in that carers, guardians and any other adults who are raising, and looking after the day-to-day needs of children and young people.

Parental engagement in schools is a relatively new phenomenon. When we were both at school, our own parents were expected to attend perhaps one parents'evening a year, and occasional events such as sports days. Today, parents are called upon to help in schools, organise social and fundraising events and to play a key role in the education process. At the very least, reading diaries need to be signed, homework supervised and assembles attended.

But not every parent can, or wants, to be involved in this process. It would be simplistic to assume that they are uninterested in their children's schooling. Many parents are unable to prioritise it while dealing with their own problems with housing, debt, substance abuse, unemployment or domestic violence. Parents in such circumstances routinely trail the baggage of their own poor experience of school, fueling distrust of teachers and the education system as a whole. And so the cycle is perpetuated.

Schools have become much better at understanding these problems, as you will read in this book, and collaboration between schools, social agencies and organisations means they are better at supporting families in difficulty.

But in recent years, 'hard to reach' has evolved to indicate more than a synonym for 'fecklessness' or 'uncaring.'

It now may also denote parents who are well-intentioned, hard-working, potentially aspirational and even middle class but just do not have as much time to devote to supporting their children's education as they might once have done, and at a time when work-life balance is a challenge for most of us. The classic example of this is attendance at the traditional parents' evening which, as we explore in Chapter 5, remains an ongoing phenomenon in home-school relationships that often satisfies neither teachers nor parents, but with which we all persevere because nothing better has been found to replace it. While it is often said that the parents teachers most want to see are those who are least likely to turn up, schools may need to be imaginative in how they organise them.

There are many excellent sources of research and insight into family learning and how parents can support their children's education directly and so, rather than focus on these, we have taken a broader, thematic approach to the issue of how to engage parents, though the overarching theme remains how to ensure children's education is prioritised in every case. Hence, there are chapters on some perhaps unexpected topics but ones which, schools have told us over the years, they have found that have brought challenges for them. Every chapter is underpinned by examples of good practice in schools that have made strides in increasing engagement, often by being innovative and responsive to parental needs. These examples won't be applicable to, or solve, every challenge in every school, but in sharing good practice we hope they will provide some insights, and perhaps help education professionals reflect on their own methods of engagement.

One chapter looks at bereavement and how, when a friend or close relative dies, schools can work with families to manage the impact on the child. Another explores the role parents can play in digital safety at a time when it is generally accepted that children are more conversant with technology than the adults around them.

With increases in mental health problems among children and young people, attributed by experts to the pressure of school, growing social and cultural challenges, and 21st-century living, we examine issues around child protection and safeguarding. And with population growth expected to result in a need for more schools in the coming years, we speak to head teachers who went about convincing parents to take a leap of faith when they set up schools from scratch.

Arguably, there is no area of education where the need for home-school collaboration is greater than in educating children with special needs and disabilities, and, in Chapter 7, we examine the complex journey teachers and parents have to negotiate jointly to find a way.

The final chapter looks at the media and we felt it was important to include this because so much of the perception of what schools are and do – and indeed, how parents are perceived – is shaped by media coverage, which today means not just the press and traditional broadcasters but the vast echo chamber that is social media.

Our primary audience for this book was always intended to be trainee teachers and others new to education, though we hope it will be of interest to everyone associated with, and working in, the education sector, whether they be heads, teachers, support staff or governors. The case studies provide some fascinating insights into life in our schools that we believe will appeal to a wider audience. As such we have not assumed great prior knowledge about how 'the system' works or about past trends, political influences or policy developments that have shaped the way our schools are run. In most cases, we've also steered clear of deconstructing why some of the problems schools face have arisen.

As journalists, and not researchers or academics, we have put together a snapshot of what's happening in schools rather than offering definitive solutions. So, each chapter starts with a narrative section outlining the theme and highlighting existing research, where applicable, before the people at the sharp end outline their stories and experiences. These include, of course, those of parents whose voices are also heard throughout each section alongside those of the professionals.

Finally, in the course of our research, we have visited, met and talked to some truly inspirational people who lead, and work in, schools in various capacities. We hope that the parents reading this book will be reassured, as we are, of their commitment to future generations, of their efforts to try to get it right and the sheer dynamism that goes into seeking to provide the best possible outcomes for children and young people, often in difficult and testing circumstances for both schools and families.

DL & JN

# 2 Bereavement

## Introduction

Death is rarely discussed. If people talked about planning for their death one tenth as much as they talk about financial, holiday or career planning, we might, as a society, be able to cope with it with more resilience when the inevitable does happen.

Most adults by the time they reach middle-age will have faced the death of someone they cared about, whether a family member or friend, and every one of the deaths is uniquely painful for that individual.

If adults find death – sudden, early or expected – difficult to face, then how much tougher is it for a child who may not even understand the concept of permanent loss, let alone know how to deal with the unfamiliar emotions or cope with the changes to routine and circumstances that the death may entail.

From a school's perspective, death and bereavement may be discussed as part of religious studies or PSHE. But, in general, it's only when a death occurs in the school community that the question of how to support the children and families involved arises. Bringing in bereavement counsellors is the expected response when the death has been traumatic for children and staff, but how should schools deal with a death when it's sad but not a crisis?

This chapter explores the impact of bereavement on children and families and looks at the challenges that arise for teachers and schools in dealing with a bereavement in their community. The resources section includes links to useful tools, research, training programmes and other materials developed by specialists such as Child Bereavement and Cruse. The tips section includes pointers for developing a bereavement policy and basic steps to support parents.

## Impact of bereavement on children

The research[1] shows a range of effects of bereavement on children. If they don't get the support needed to help them deal with a death, emotionally, mentally and practically, it affects their attainment, achievement and their physical health, and it means time off school and time visiting a doctor as well as a melee of behavioural and emotional responses.

Kari Dyregrov and Atle Dyregrov identified frequent reactions that include anxiety, vivid memories, difficulties in sleeping, sadness and longing, anger and acting out behaviour, guilt, self-reproach and shame, school problems and physical complaints. Less common reactions were regressive behaviour, social isolation, fantasies, personality changes, pessimism about the future, preoccupation with cause and meaning and a sense of maturation and growth as a result of being bereaved.[2]

However they respond at the time, the experience of bereavement is likely to have an impact on the child later on. If bereavement happens when they are young, when they may respond pragmatically, and their understanding of it is likely to change as they develop cognitively so it might not be until they are 15 or 16 when everyone else's Mum is buying a prom dress, when they go to university or the realisation hits that Dad won't be there to walk them down the aisle, that a huge emotional response is triggered.

Researchers have pointed to reducing parental distress as one of a set of tactics and strategies for helping children deal with bereavement. In one family bereavement programme in the US "Parents were taught that while they did not need to hide their distress from their children, they should try to reassure their child . . . that although they are sad and upset now, that they or the family is strong and will get through this with time."[3]

Including services for parents and carers and creating services that build family cohesion and adaptability to loss are also listed by Stokes[4] as priorities for practitioners striving to build children's resilience in the face of bereavement.

## Ways of grieving

The charity Child Bereavement UK supports children, schools, families and professionals in coping with death and bereavement.

Assistant Director of Bereavement Services and Education at Child Bereavement UK, Dr Katie Koehler, says that one challenge for teachers striving to support families where a child has been bereaved is that everyone is likely to be grieving in a different way.

> Grief is a very individual thing and sometimes it can seem as if the parents want something slightly different from what the child wants. Parents may be struggling with how to talk about how the person died, particularly if it is a traumatic death. However, children need a simple explanation for what has happened. Usually, what happens is that they are given partial information and often that's because the adults around them are trying to be very protective.
>
> (Katie Koehler, Assistant Director of Bereavement Services, Child Bereavement UK, June 2018)

There may be an added layer of complication if the parents are divorced, she points out.

> How a child responds when a parent dies is dependent on many factors, including the nature of the child's relationship with the person who has died. This may well be complex in the case of families where contact may have been limited and loyalties may have been divided. How the remaining parent responds is crucial for any child bereaved of a parent, whether or not they were separated/divorced, as children will take their lead from how the adults around them are responding.

Some deaths attract particular attention beyond the family. In suicide cases, parents' instinct is often to shield children from the harsh truth that people may choose to take their own lives, yet it may swiftly become common knowledge among the school community once an inquest has been held and the information is in the public domain.

Schools are always treading a fine line because if they have information that the child doesn't know, it's not up to them to share it. Similarly, teachers may have a different view of what is in the best interests of the child in other respects.

> A parent might say "Oh, I think Tommy is too young to come to the funeral, he's only seven," whereas the teacher might think "Actually, I think at seven he's capable of going, and it might help him understand a bit more about what's happened and the reality of the fact that this person is not coming back." It could be that the parent is worried about 'managing' a younger child during the funeral service so there might be practical things that the teacher could suggest – someone could accompany the child or they could be given some colouring to do in a corner, which could be fine. So it's about helping the parents make an informed choice.
>
> What's important in all of these instances is to have that conversation with the parent, keeping the communication and open dialogue available so you are "not alienating parents by just giving your own views, but helping them to come to the decision that is right for them."

## Death of a parent or carer

If it is the child's parent or carer who has died, the loss will affect them in a range of ways and school can be a valuable point of constancy at a time of turmoil.

"If a parent or carer dies, it might be very practical things that the child focuses on first," Dr Koehler says.

> We know that children are affected by all of the secondary losses that happen when there's a death so it's not just the loss of the emotional attachment to the person who has died but all of those things

that might change – who's going to take me to school, who's going to take me to football – and sometimes for children those things can be big things so they are not to be underestimated. At the same time, the surviving parent may well not be 'there' in an emotional sense because they are dealing with their own grief and it's difficult for them to be providing for the emotional needs of the children in the family.

But whereas at home the whole emotional environment is affected, at school in can be a bit of an oasis of normality. It's predictable, it's consistent and the same rules of behaviour still apply so the child has the same boundaries so there's reassurance in that consistency.

## Risks for teachers

While they are supporting a bereaved family, the danger for some teachers is that they become too involved, which may be disruptive in itself and/or may bring to the surface from their own childhood experiences of death and bereavement.

"It's true that everyone has their own risk points and vulnerabilities and you don't know when they are going to pop up so heads do need to be aware of this," Dr Koehler says.

> I don't think that it's a problem if teachers show their emotion, their humanity, in being upset by something. The problem comes when they are in floods of tears and more upset than the parent or child they are trying to reassure, so it is something that heads would have to be aware of that and not underestimate. Even if someone has the greatest self-awareness in the world, sometimes seeing a child bereaved can trigger things from their own childhood.

## Learning about death

Should death be on the curriculum? It is for secondary schools in England in the context of GCSE Religious Studies but mainly in relation to beliefs about life after death and the rituals associated with death, or in the death penalty as a discussion topic in ethics.[5] In terms of PSHE, guidance from the PSHE Association includes content on bereavement under health and well-being and relationships at KS2, KS3 and KS4. In Scotland, the Curriculum for Excellence references bereavement under inclusion and supporting children with different needs, while in Northern Ireland, it is referenced as part of religious education. (See further resources.)

Individual agencies and schools have developed their own resources for incorporating death and bereavement into the curriculum. In Scotland, A Whole School Approach to Supporting Loss and Bereavement (2013), produced by Glasgow City Council, contains information and advice to help staff support bereaved young people and children and includes case studies and ideas for activities involving parents. (See further resources.)

But should death be dealt with more explicitly? The case has been made in the past for making a wider and deeper understanding about death, dying and bereavement a part of the secondary curriculum by organisations such as Dying Matters,[6] which was established in 2009 by the National Council for Palliative Care to promote awareness of death and bereavement.

Dr Koehler believes death could be and should be included as a theme or subject in the curriculum at a primary and secondary level. It would not lessen the shock or grief when a death occurs, but it could help make children, families and staff more resilient and able to process and deal with the impact of the loss and its ripple effects.

> Our experience at Child Bereavement UK is that that teachers can lack confidence in dealing with bereavement which means that they sometimes shy away from it and don't talk about it. But teaching children about death would give children an understanding of what their peers who have been bereaved may be experiencing in terms of emotion, as well as preparing them in some small way for when they experience bereavement themselves. It would show them that it's OK to talk about it.

In particular, says Dr Koehler, it would be useful to address the language around bereavement so that children are in no doubt when a death has occurred. The sensitivity around death can sometimes confuse or mislead children, well intentioned though it is.

> Because we want to protect children, we don't give them the language that they need. I looked up how many different euphemisms there are for how to avoid saying 'dead' and in the English language there are well over 80 ways to avoid using the words dead or died. And people do use them! I can spend all day training people and talking about the importance of language and how we need to use the words 'dead' and 'died' with children rather than 'passed on' or 'passed away' or 'lost' and at the end of the day, someone will still come and say 'Oh, I just want to ask you about this. It was so and so who passed away' – it's entrenched.

(Of course, families' own choices still need to be respected and if they are referring to grandma 'passing away' it shouldn't be challenged. It's in the classroom that clarity is preferable.)

> Many parents we support whose child, sadly, has died, are still very careful about what they say to other people. People will ask them how many children they have, for example, and they say "Oh, I didn't like to say two but one's died, so I said one and then I felt bad because it felt disrespectful to the one who has died but I didn't dare say that I had two because then there would be the conversation I would have to have."

Younger children, in particular, who are less inhibited about language, may ask the blunt "Who has died? How did they die? What will happen to them?" questions anyway. Yet they take their cues from the adults around them and if the adults are not talking about it, then children very quickly realise it's something that they mustn't mention, because it upsets people.

> If they know that everyone else is using euphemisms, rather than saying 'died,' that tells them that it's a no-go area, that you shouldn't ask questions and you shouldn't talk about it. It closes them down.

> In a way, the emotional aspects of bereavement can be less of a challenge than getting the language right. But it's just about answering children's questions and being honest. If you do that, you are giving them a narrative that makes sense that you haven't got to undo in a few years' time.

It's especially important to be clear in language with children with additional needs. A child on the autism spectrum, for example, may not understand directly or from the context phrases such as 'passed away.'

> Your average neuro-typical child will eventually pick up that passed away means died and they can relate to it. For children with additional needs, that's much, much harder. So it makes it harder for children to really understand what's going on and also to feel open about sharing how they feel.

All of that said, and even though clarity is recommended, teachers still need to remain sensitive to each situation and take note of the family's approach. Again, schools do have to tread a careful line and they have to find out what vocabulary the family are using and use that. If it's appropriate – if the communication with the family is good, then you can have a discussion with them about how they phrase things.

Overall, most bereaved children just need some very simple measures put in place, Dr Koehler says, which means the adults around them knowing a bit about the normal response to grief and understanding the things that they can do to support children.

"There are few who will need specialist services or additional support through other agencies such as counselling services or CAMHS, and if it's dealt with effectively and with the support of adults around, most children will continue to thrive."

## Training and policy

Cruse, the bereavement support charity, works closely with schools and provides training for staff in how to support young people when a death happens in the school. Its course on the impact of bereavement on children and young people covers a range of topics including cognitive understanding of bereavement at different stages and ages and how children react to death.

A whole-school approach to training is critical, says Alison Thomas who leads on the work for schools in Wales. "Generally, if school teachers, staff, secretaries, dinner staff, everyone associated with the school, hasn't had any training in the impact of bereavement, it will be difficult for them to handle when it happens, so training is key."

Creating a school policy on bereavement gives staff more confidence in dealing with bereavement. In effect, a framework that has been agreed avoids people feeling like they have to 'make it up' when a bereavement does happen and they know the steps to take to ensure support is in place and is right. But the act of devising the policy also raises awareness of the issue, giving staff 'permission' to discuss death from different perspectives, emotional as well as practically. Reviewing the existing policy, if there is one, is a good way to kick-start the whole-school conversation.

As with the training, Cruse recommends involving all members of the school staff team, not just senior leaders, to develop the policy, although leadership is important.

> If the head understands bereavement and 'gets it,' then the culture of that school is going to be very different from one led by a head who doesn't have a proper understanding of it or who perhaps believes children will 'get over it' – whose approach is 'throw them back in and they'll be fine.' And very often they are not. Their grief is just as deep and as hurtful and difficult to deal with as an adult.
>
> (Alison Thomas, Children and Young People's Service and Development Manager, Cruse, May 2018)

How do you start the conversation? Look at your existing policy, put one in place if there isn't one and get the staff involved in developing it. Use the schools pack, get an expert in from a specialist organisation, like Cruse, get the training scheduled into the school inset training programme, if you can. Talk to the university to get something written into course programme PG so that it's core to the course. I believe it should be a core element in every course.

In the longer term, communication between people involved with a family through a child's school career can head off problems that may be years in the making.

"The transfer of information between primary and secondary schools needs to include details of any bereavement that a child may have experienced," Alison Thomas says.

> If communication from primary to secondary doesn't include, for example, that a child's mum died when he was nine or there have been multiple bereavements in a family then on trigger dates, like Mother's Day or Father's Day or birthdays, the behaviour of those children may change. So it's vital that information is passed from school to school. It sounds like common sense but it is dependent on paperwork, processes and people being mindful of that, of putting it on the agenda.

(See case study – Jess and Paula.)

## Incidence of bereavement for children

Research by Alison Penny and Di Stubbs[7] for the Child Bereavement Network drew together statistics and information related to bereavement in childhood and its effects includes estimates for the number of children who deal with a death each year.

How many young children and young people say they have been bereaved?

In a sample of 11–16 year olds (secondary school) in the north-west of England:

- 78% said they had been bereaved of a close relative or close friend

(*continued*)

## Incidence of bereavement for children (*continued*)

- 92% said they had been bereaved of a close relative friend or pet.

(Harrison and Harrington 2001)

What proportion of deaths are sudden or unexpected?

> At least 25 per cent of deaths in England and Wales are unexpected deaths from sudden causes. However, many patients with chronic/long-term conditions also die unexpectedly, which would push the figure for 'unexpected' deaths up. It could be as high as 42 per cent.
>
> (Blackmore and others, 2011 UK)

Are some children more likely to be bereaved than others?

Ribbens McCarthy and Jessop (2005) point out that life expectancy varies by social class and geography. For example, Manchester has a death rate among people under 75 almost 2.3 times higher than that of Wokingham. This variation is due to differences in risk factors, such as obesity, alcohol and smoking and socio-economic determinants (Public Health England 2013)

This means that some adults and children are more likely to die early and therefore some children and young people are more likely to be bereaved. Gaps in life expectancy in the UK are widening (ONS 2011).

## Bereaved children – physical health

Around 13% of children had somatic [physical] symptoms in the clinical range during the first year after the death, compared to

(*continued*)

## Bereaved children – physical health (*continued*)

around 4% of non-bereaved children. Girls were more affected than boys (Worden, 1996 US).

Bereaved children were more likely than non-bereaved to experience a serious illness by the end of the first year since bereavement: 70% of bereaved children reported mild illness (Worden, 1996 US).

Thirty-four per cent of bereaved children experienced accidents during the first year post-bereavement compared with 26% of non-bereaved (Worden, 1996 US).

Fauth and others (2009 UK) found that children who had been bereaved were also more likely to have had a serious illness requiring hospitalisation at some point in their childhood (it might have been before bereavement).

Source: CBN Bereavement in Childhood – What do we know in 2015

## Death on the curriculum

Sally Paul, a lecturer in social work, was part of a team who undertook research with the universities of Edinburgh and Strathclyde to explore and develop practice in dealing with death and bereavement with primary schools.[8] It grew out of Sally's previous career as a social worker running child bereavement services.

"We were getting lots of referrals and they weren't always necessary and where it would have been possible for the bereavement needs to have been managed by people already known to the young person, rather than referring them for specialist support," she says. "That was a concern because it was pathologising

(*continued*)

### Death on the curriculum (*continued*)

bereavement as a medical problem which only specialists could deal with."

The research explored the role schools could play in helping to normalise bereavement and in educating children about death as part of that normalisation. Sally spoke to children at two schools in years P6 and 7 (9–12 years) about what they wanted to know about death and its impact. "The children were curious about what happens to dead bodies, does your hair still grow, can you see, is heaven real, what happens to your soul, why do some people get buried and some cremated, what's organ donation," Sally says.

They then produced ideas for practice to advance education and support around death and bereavement. This included developing training for school staff, a schools bereavement policy and a death and grief education programme. One school, St Francis Xavier's in Falkirk, developed a curriculum called the Resilience Project that involved teaching the children about loss and death as part of the lifecycle and included homework tasks which involved parents. One task focussed on remembrance and involved children taking home a cross and talking to their parents about someone in the family who had died, writing the person's name on the cross, and posting it on a remembrance wall back in a corridor at school. It was a good way of stimulating conversation among other children who were interested to see the wall and the names on it, as well as to create an opportunity for families to discuss death at home. Another work task looked at funeral customs which the children could research at home alongside parents and carers.

"Teachers we spoke to covered funeral customs when they did the Egyptians for example, but they might not mention death specifically and children said the same: death in history lessons wasn't really mentioned or loss acknowledged and grief wasn't touched on," Sally says. "It was the same in literature: death was

(*continued*)

### Death on the curriculum (*continued*)

never the teaching focus. The children said they wanted to learn about death and that doing it when it wasn't personal was helpful. Tasks like the funeral customs one do make death the focus but it's not personal so the children can learn about it objectively."

Generally, the research found that staff did not lack the skills to deal with bereavement and death but did lack the confidence in how to go about addressing the topics.

Simple training in bereavement and an opportunity to develop staff's confidence would be really important in helping them acknowledge the fact of a bereavement with a child. But in terms of education, it needs to be more than 'bereavement.' It would help if schools educated children about death as part of the lifespan, so that it would not be unusual to talk about bereavement as a natural part of that discussion. And there are lots of ways schools can incorporate it, it doesn't need to be a separate programme. Children are taught about the caterpillar going into its cocoon and emerging as a butterfly but not that it will live for a few years and then die, so death is not included in their understanding of the lifespan. But that would be an easy way to introduce death and grief as a topic in a way that is entirely natural and not personal.

(Sally Paul, Strathclyde, Lecturer in Social Work,
School of Social Work and Social Policy,
University of Strathclyde, July 2018)

### Case study: 'Jess and Paula'

When she was 11 and not long after she started secondary school, Jess [not her real name], received a shattering phone call. Her 53-year-old dad had died of a heart attack.

(*continued*)

## Case study: 'Jess and Paula' (*continued*)

Her parents had been divorced since she was three and she lived with her mum but she had a good relationship with her dad and his unexpected death was naturally a shock to her system.

"It completely changed the way I acted and behaved," recalls Jess, now 17 and an A level student. "Before my dad died I was a confident person, always willing to talk. After his death, I became more quiet and shy. It made me more closed off and unsure of myself and my decisions. The fact is I didn't know how to react or respond to the situation that I was in.

"I was at a new school, I didn't know any of the teachers well enough and didn't really have a close group of friends because everyone was still getting to know each other. My brother, who is a year older, was in a similar situation but he had been at his school for a year so he knew the teachers well and had a close group of friends. And as my parents had been divorced since I was three, my mum was not grieving for my dad in quite the same way."

Feeling isolated, Jess's unhappiness was compounded by a bad experience when she returned to school.

> I took a few days off school to grieve and spend time with my family but on the first day that I was back at school, I had a meeting with my mum and my head of year. We went in to the school and the person in the office said "Oh are you here to see matron because she is very busy so you won't be able to, sorry," but I felt she said it in a rude way which made me feel as though my grief wasn't important.
>
> (Jess and Paula (pseudonyms), July 2018)

Paula, Jess's mum, says one member of staff thought her daughter's late return to school was because the family had been on holiday. "She was shocked when I told her it was actually

(*continued*)

## Case study: 'Jess and Paula' (*continued*)

because Jess's dad had died. The head of year then told me that Jess was 'fine' because her classmates and the teachers had been told what had happened plus she had been told how to access counselling online – so that was all OK!"

Jess was offered face-to-face counselling at school but says the approach was insensitive, again because the counsellor had not been properly apprised of the situation.

> When I went to my counselling session I walked in and the lady told me to tell her exactly what had happened to me which I felt was wrong as I knew she must [have] some of the information already. I could not bring myself to tell a stranger what had happened to me just like that and the experience put me off counsellors. I haven't been to see one since because of this experience.

After drawing a blank with the school, Paula contacted Child Bereavement UK and the school subsequently formed a link with the charity, too.

"I complained to the head about how the situation had been handled and the head was very apologetic but the damage had been done by then. The school is now working with Child Bereavement UK, so some good did come out of it."

Jess says: "I don't think the school understood what to do and there was not enough communication between members of staff at the school, so it felt like I was alone and like nobody cared. I think it would be useful if teachers had some sort of training on how to deal specifically with bereavement because obviously it is a tough subject and quite complicated to deal with. But I also think that it would be useful if schools did recognise bereavement as an important subject, perhaps as part of PSHE, because I do

(*continued*)

## Case study: 'Jess and Paula' (*continued*)

feel that it comes under the umbrella of mental health. I feel as though it could be very beneficial if bereavement was a topic that was covered in these sessions to give people an insight into what to do if someone close to them is bereaved."

Although the experience didn't knock Jess off-track and she is now 17 and aiming for university, it resurfaces from time to time, showing just how far-reaching the impact of bereavement can be.

> I was in a Spanish exam in year 10, three years after my dad's death, and I was asked who was in my family and I answered that it was my mum, my brother and I. The next question was then "What job does your dad do?" which completely threw me off-balance. I received a low mark which my teacher was not impressed with as Spanish is something I am good at. My mum phoned the school and this teacher later apologised but it did affect my grade for that one exam.

## Case study: Jo Laker, head teacher, Braithwaite Primary School, Keswick

Jo Laker has been head of Braithwaite Primary School in Keswick for 11 years, including a period where a number of families were bereaved in a short period. She discusses this in the following:

I've probably dealt with four or five families who have lost a parent in varying circumstances in the time I have been here, which is quite unusual for a small school of 50–100 children. In some circumstances we knew there was an impending death which, in some ways, is easier to prepare for but in others is still

(*continued*)

## Case study: Jo Laker, head teacher, Braithwaite Primary School, Keswick (*continued*)

as hard because it's drawn out over a longer period. Others have been sudden and unexpected which presents other challenges.

One of the difficulties staff have faced is dealing with deeply upset parents in a small community and helping them to communicate why they are upset to their own children. In one case, a parent who died was also a helper at the school and known to everyone so staff, parents and children were all very affected and felt it very sharply, while the staff were also dealing with the impact on the child.

We have an understanding with staff in terms of how we deal with these things now. It's largely about communicating with parents, the school community and between staff, and making sure that we are acting in line with what parents have asked us to do. For example, in one family we knew of the death before the child, so it was very important that this was kept confidential until it had been communicated to the people who needed to know first.

In other cases, when we know mum or dad isn't going to get better, we talk to the family about whether or not (and when) they want us to say anything to other children and families in the school, so that there is some measure of understanding of the situation.

Sometimes, other parents and children might want to do fundraising as a way of showing their support but while some families are grateful for the support, others may feel uncomfortable with it so the school can act as the conduit and relay the family's wishes to the community.

A very practical way in which we can help the bereaved family is in giving the child an understanding of what happens at a funeral. If a child returns to school before the funeral, and this is

(*continued*)

### Case study: Jo Laker, head teacher, Braithwaite Primary School, Keswick (*continued*)

often the case with a relative who is a bit further removed from them, such as a grandparent, then I will try to make time to talk to a child about a funeral before they go, with the parents' permission. Sometimes families do not discuss it and the child may not know what to expect so it can be overwhelming for them. It's easier for us if we don't know the grandparent to talk about the 'box' and the fact there will be a body in it. If a child is going to be part of the funeral in any way, such as putting something on the grave, we can help to prepare the child. These are the sorts of things as adults sometimes we assume children know but and they don't. It's also helpful to know what families have said to the child, particularly in terms of religious beliefs (e.g. grandma has gone to heaven) so that the school can follow the same lead.

We had an instance where a mum came in after her child's father had died suddenly and she wanted us to help her to help her child. what she should say and not say. In particular, she wasn't sure whether the child should go to the funeral. We talked gently about the importance of telling a child the truth and what would be age-appropriate to her child. But we also said it's important not to put the onus for decision-making on children about things like whether or not to go to a funeral, partly because they may do what they think the adult wants them to do. It's better if adults listen to the child and what they want but then make the big decisions, such as attending a funeral or seeing a family member when very ill; ultimately the child shouldn't be pushed to make the big decision for themselves.

If I thought a parent wasn't handling a situation well for a child, perhaps if they refused to answer the child's questions, then I would try to talk to the parent about how to approach

(*continued*)

## Case study: Jo Laker, head teacher, Braithwaite Primary School, Keswick (*continued*)

it. My advice to the parent is, if the child asks direct questions about it, try to be truthful in the answers. This would be especially important if others in the community already knew about the death and the circumstances, as may well happen. As staff, we would not want to risk our relationship with the child by telling them something that is evidently not the case so you are treading a line between respecting the parents' views at a very emotional time and trying to do what is best for the child. But it does depend on the situation. If they really believe that they don't want the child to go to the funeral, you have to respect their views.

When we had the series of deaths in quick succession in the school community, it caused anxiety among some children who started to worry about mummy or daddy dying; they became anxious about parents not going out, not being left with babysitters and them not coming back. We put some information in our school newsletter signposting parents to websites such as Child Bereavement UK where they could find advice to help them talk to their children about it. Obviously, you can never say to a child, it's never going to happen to us but what you can talk to them about what has happened and reassure them that it's unlikely to be the case for you.

If a child has lost a parent we would not expect them to return to the school until after the funeral, so our policy is to visit them at home before they return to school, ideally before the funeral, or at least have a meeting with the family. We talk to them about how they feel about returning to school and what we say to the other children. We also talk about any school staff attending the funeral so the family are not thrown by this. We say that it's OK to be upset about these things and will talk about that again

(*continued*)

> **Case study: Jo Laker, head teacher, Braithwaite Primary School, Keswick** (*continued*)
>
> when that child returns to school, giving the child strategies for if they get upset and need to leave the classroom, for example, and how to deal with questions from peers. We also encourage staff to acknowledge the death to the child when they see the child, for example, saying something privately to them about being sad to hear about the death but glad to see the child back in school.
>
> It's difficult but it is important because I think children's early experiences of death can have a profound effect and if it's done 'well' as it were, and if they are supported through it, chances of it having a negative effect on them later on are much reduced, I think.

## Writing a bereavement policy

### *Writing a bereavement policy: general points*

- Identify a person to lead and implement the work. Encompass all the school staff, including support staff, in its development so the awareness runs right through the school.
- Organise training for all concerned.
- Look at other schools' examples of bereavement policy and see if they can be adapted to your context.
- Include a simple flow chart of actions in your school bereavement policy.
- Make sure that the plans in place reflect medium and longer term needs, as well as 'crisis' points. For example, do you have a mechanism for ensuring that information about a child's bereavement follows when the child moves from primary to secondary school?

### *Writing a bereavement policy – parents and carers*

- Contact with the deceased's family should be established by the head and their wishes respected in communicating with others.
- Determine who will be responsible for communicating with the families directly involved. The head may be the point of contact for the family but the child may prefer to talk to or see their class teacher, not the head.
- Identify who will give the news to the rest of the school community. In terms of breaking sad news to pupils and families, make sure you have the facts to share and think through how to obtain factual information to prevent rumours and assumptions spreading.
- A letter should go to families the same day if possible. A pre-prepared script is helpful as finding the right form of words is more difficult under pressure.
- Consider including guidelines for parents on supporting bereaved children with the letter.
- Review your policy from time to time as the thinking on how to support bereaved children and families, emotionally and practically, can change.

Sources: https://childbereavementuk.org/for-schools/training-for-schools/, www.cruse.org.uk/for-schools/bereavement-policy

## Resources

### *Key organisations*

Child Bereavement UK – https://childbereavementuk.org

Supports bereaved children, young people and their families across the UK and features many teaching resources for professionals, such as Elephant's Tea Party (www.elephantsteaparty.co.uk), resources for primary schools, which uses elephants and their life-cycle to help children learn about death and dying in a non-threatening way. Training packages include workshops on supporting parents and families and can be tailored to schools' needs.

Cruse Bereavement Care – www.cruse.org.uk

Cruse supports anyone who has been bereaved and offers loss and bereavement awareness training for teachers and other professionals on how to support young people and recognising the impact of bereavement on families. Its Hope Again website (www.hopeagain.org.uk) offers advice and online support for young people dealing with a death from other young people who have been bereaved. It includes family stories which follow three families through the grieving process and short films.

### *Other*

Dying Matters – www.dyingmatters.org/page/lesson-plan-resources

This coalition of groups including NHS organisations, voluntary groups, charities, hospices and care homes was established in 2009 and has resources to help start conversations about death and bereavement, including lesson plan and PowerPoint.

Glasgow City Council Education Services – *A whole school approach to supporting loss and bereavement* www.seemescotland.org/media/8151/whole_school_approach_to_lossandbereavement.pdf

A toolkit to help staff widen their knowledge and understanding of bereavement, loss and change.

JN

## Notes

1 CBN Bereavement in Childhood: What do we know?
2 The Role of Family, Friends, Colleagues, Schools and Support Professionals Kari Dyregrov and Atle Dyregrov, 2008
3 Haine and others 2008, US, via CBN Bereavement in Childhood 2015.

4 Stokes, J. (2009) Resilience and bereaved children, *Bereavement Care*, 28(1), 9–17, DOI: 10.1080/02682620902746078
5 Religious studies GCSE subject content. February 2015 https://assets.publishing.service.gov.uk/government/uploads/system/uploads/attachment_data/file/403357/GCSE_RS_final_120215.pdf
6 https://www.dyingmatters.org/
7 CBN Bereavement in Childhood: What do we know?
8 Integrating palliative care into the community: the role of hospices and schools, Paul, Sally; Cree, Viviene E; Murray, Scott A, https://pure.strath.ac.uk/portal/en/publications/integrating-palliative-care-into-the-community(c695f162-f43b-4fe5-99c1-63316888a2ed).html

# 3 Digital safety

## Introduction

The impact of the internet on children's lives – its threats and opportunities – is a key parental concern. A few figures from the annual Ofcom report[1] into families' use of the media highlight just how closely it is woven into children's lives today:

- By age four 53% of children use the internet.
- Eight in ten 12–15 year olds own a smartphone.
- About 74% of 12–15 year olds and 23% of 8–11 year olds have social media profiles.

And these figures have risen year on year.

Safety online is also high on schools' agendas. Cyberbullying, sexting, culture and other aspects of social media on children's mental health and the grooming threat are just some of the issues schools and parents have grappled with for many years. Social media has ramped up the pressure with its culture of 'likes' and images, while the popularity of YouTube – with children keen to emulate the vloggers they follow and create their own channel – and the introduction of live streaming has presented further challenges. Both parents and teachers may struggle to keep up to speed with children who seem so at ease with the use of technology and appear to absorb new technologies into their lives almost instinctively. In 2017, Ofcom reported that one in six parents of 12–15 year olds feel they don't know enough to help their child manage online risks[2] (Ofcom, 2017). Meanwhile, the British Educational Suppliers Association (BESA) surveyed 1,325 ICT leaders in UK schools and found that 51% of primary school teachers and 49% of secondary school teachers needed training in e-safety.[3]

Sometimes, concern about these issues even overshadows the learning, communication and collaboration opportunities that technology provides.

Yet despite this awareness, engaging parents in learning about digital safety and the steps they can take to ensure their children are equipped to deal with the potential risks is something that schools have found particularly hard to tackle, says David Wright, director of the UK Safer Internet Centre, the key body in the UK for overseeing safety issues for schools and families:

> It's definitely a challenge for schools to engage parents. Whether that's because parents don't appreciate the risks or there's a lethargy around safety is not clear but it continues to be an issue.
>
> The parents that we see at our sessions with schools are not necessarily representative of the school population as a whole – they are the ones who engage regularly anyway – and although we are seeing a general increase in interest, it's still low. The idea of technology as the 'electronic babysitter' which occupies children and gives busy parents some quiet time themselves, rather than something that parents need to be taking an active role in, is one that still prevails.
>
> (David Wright, Director, UK Safer Internet Centre, March 2018)

This chapter looks at ways in which schools and others have engaged parents in digital safety and in particular how working and learning with their but also from their children has proved a powerful way to draw in parents who might otherwise be hard to reach.

See also Chapter 9: Media.

## Background: policy and regulation

In 2008, Professor Tanya Byron produced a government-commissioned report on child safety online, *Safer Children in a Digital World*, which was intended to set a framework for government action. It made 38 recommendations, including better information and education about e-safety and the creation of the UK Council for Child Internet Safety.

In the decade since, technology has leapt forward with the growth of social media, the widespread take-up of the smartphone and mobile internet access. In 2018, the NSPCC reviewed the Byron recommendations and looked at the wider changes in technology and society that have an impact on children's safety online.

It concluded that several of the Byron recommendations had not been addressed fully. The government had not specified online safety as a priority for teachers' continuing professional development and, while newly qualified teachers must take a digital safety ICT test, confidence in experienced teachers is low with 51% of primary school teachers, and 49% of secondary school teachers, seem to require training in e-safety issues.[4]

Recommendations on tighter controls on the gaming industry, such as raising standards on parental controls on games or the idea of parental consoles being switched on as a standard on all new games consoles, had not been taken up either.

Perhaps most surprisingly, the Byron Report's call for an evaluation of the way online safety was taught in schools, especially primary, simply did not happen.

However, the NSPCC review was more optimistic about efforts to introduce an online safety and conduct aspect into relationship and sex education, under the Children and Social Work Act 2017 (CSWA).

In its conclusion, the NSPCC review called for a renewed policy ambition on digital safety to include more children knowing how to keep themselves safe online and more adults knowing how to keep children safe online.

Some other measures have made a difference. The Bailey report[5] in 2011, which stipulated to internet providers that they should enable parents to make an active choice when it comes to setting parental controls on online technologies, and the introduction of network level filters, did lead to a small rise in the number of parents using parental controls (from 50% to 54%) and it has risen again since (the filters are provided for free by most internet service providers).

David Wright also points to age verification measures included in the Digital Economy Act 2017, which means that internet providers of 'commercial adult content' (pornography, for the most part) worldwide will be required to verify that the user is over 18 by more sophisticated means than a tick box, are also likely to have an impact, although the Act will not extend to social media.

> In one month in 2017, 27 million people in the UK are estimated to have accessed adult content online, according to figures from the British Board of Film Classification, and 1.5m of them are thought to be children. So that's what these latest measures are meant to address. The BBFC has said it will go after advertising revenues if the provider doesn't comply so that's an incentive for them to comply.
>
> For us, it has great merit for younger children, for those with mild curiosity or are accidentally exposed to this sort of content but the one thing we always say is it will not stop a teenager with intent. And it may drive traffic to sites on social media where sites are not covered by the act.

## Does 'prevention' work?

For many parents, digital safety has meant, in essence, limiting children's access to the internet because exposure/over-exposure to it is thought to be harmful – the protection strategy. This is so even when children are being taught to be savvy online and be alert to the inappropriate behaviour of a fellow online gamer or spot a website offering an 'alternative' version of history in which the Germans won World War II. But technology is now so deeply embedded in children's lives that insisting they only use it at certain times or for specific purposes may be counterproductive – i.e., children learn less and take greater risks – and possibly unenforceable, research suggests.

> For many years, research has predominantly examined parental efforts to restrict or reduce media exposure or mitigate its negative effects by enhancing children's critical media literacy, and policy advice has followed suit. While protection remains important, such advice is insufficient to meet growing expectations of children's digital media use in relation to learning, employment, communication, and participation.[6]

A study in 2016 into how parents act as mediators for their children's online experience concluded that it may be time to "rethink the dominant emphasis on harm in parental mediation research and parenting advice"[7] and that finding ways to improve the digital skills of parents and children could help parents to embrace a wider range of opportunities for their kids online while also helping to reduce the risk of exposure to harm. Make everyone more digital and online-confident, in other words, and they will be safer and get more than ever out of the online world.

The same research also found that the assumption that better-educated parents were more adept in the online world was wrong, as was the belief that younger parents are more digitally skilled. Traci Good, an online safety consultant, EPICT trainer and 360 Safe assessor with a background in safeguarding and youth work, works closely with schools and parents – as well as local authorities and the police – to raise awareness of good e-safety practice.

The schools are in a range of socio-economic circumstances, from poor areas to fee-paying independent and boarding schools, and Traci has found that, in general, parents at schools in poorer areas tend to be most knowledgeable about e-safety risks.

"When we go into schools in areas where there are high levels of deprivation, parents are probably more street smart and know what to look out for so they can often keep their children safer because they understand some of the stuff that goes on," she says.

"Whereas the children of parents who are money rich and time poor often have access to fantastic devices but the adults don't have the time or inclination to ensure they stay safe. The whole world of grooming and that sort of thing is just so far removed from their own reality that they don't see it as being an issue."

The rapid rate at which technology moves on also means that even those young parents who may themselves be termed 'digital natives' aren't automatically attuned to online risks that have emerged in recent years.

"Parents in their twenties, for example, have grown up with mobile internet at their disposal as teenagers but not with platforms such as Snapchat or with live streaming. As a result, they may base their own assumptions and expectations of their children's behaviour too much on their own experience, rather than the current reality."

## Children on social media

Parents may not know too much about what their children do online and may not know how to find out anyway. With social media, for example, while preteens should not be using the apps, the reality is that plenty of them are.

One primary school teacher, where digital safety is embedded across the curriculum, says that children at the school tend to use Snapchat and WhatsApp for conversations and Instagram for sharing and liking things. YouTube is also a very popular medium they use as well, but they see Facebook as 'for old people, parents.'

With Instagram, for example, children love the app partly because a lot of celebrities are on it and it has a big reach but also because kids love selfies and they want likes, the teacher says. "They want to share their lives with people and for a lot of them, their world is driven the like culture."

And while most of the parents are aware the children are using it, they assume it is locked down, i.e., the posts are not publicly viewable. This school takes the approach that it is better to help children use the platform safely – at home as well as school – rather than try to ban them from using it. One teacher reported:

> We know that it's probably impossible to stop them using it so our job is to make sure they know how to use it safely. What

are they posting and is it appropriate? Are their accounts locked down or open to the whole world? What comments are they posting on the pictures and are they appropriate? Would someone else construe it in a different manner from what the pupil intended?

If we find a pupil is not being safe – if they are using their real name, for example, or the account is open to the whole world – then I speak to them and email their parents to let them know. It's important that the child knows we're not just talking about safe behaviour in school but at home and everywhere else too.

Peer pressure will drive children's enthusiasm for apps like Snapchat and WhatsApp: they want to be part of the gang communicating this way, something that parents may find difficult to grasp, having not grown up with these apps themselves, she says.

Parents don't particularly want the children to have them but it is children's way of communicating. Rather than picking up the phone and talking for hours on end, they message and photo each other until the late hours. Parents don't like it and want to know how we can stop it. And I say, we can't stop it for you but we can help you to manage it and make it safer for them.

"Different technologies present different challenges," Traci Good adds.

Snapchat is likely to be around for a long time, like Facebook and Instagram, and parents and teachers need to be aware how the children are using it. Its Snapmaps facility, for example, uses GPS to show other users where someone is in real time.

This facility has its uses; as a parent, you would know whether a child really had gone to the shop, for example, but it is clearly open to abuse by others, she says.

From a parent's perspective, if your kids tell you they are going to McDonald's and you can see that they have actually gone into the town instead, it's great – you can keep tabs on your children.

> From a grooming perspective, however, it's terrifying. It's incredibly easy to turn off the GPS by going into the settings – it puts you into 'ghost mode' – but you need to know that it's necessary.
>
> (Traci Good, online safety consultant, July 2018)

Parents need to know who is on their child's friends lists so they know who they might be sharing their location with, she recommends. It's also important for a parent or carer to know how to block and report within an app and then ensure that their children can do it, too, because the adult won't always be present.

"As with all parenting we need to give our children the skills to make safe choices and hope they will do that."

## Getting parents in

The big challenge for many schools is how to get parents through the doors; busy mums and dads are often unable or unwilling to spare the time to attend yet another school talk.

ChildNet, the e-safety specialist body, runs a number of initiatives to promote digital safety to children, schools and families, and coordinates the annual Internet Safety Day every February. It has a team that goes into schools, giving talks to children as young as three, for staff and also running sessions for parents and parental engagement is the issue that schools find most difficult, says ChildNet chief executive Will Gardner:

> It's a challenge because parents are, by definition busy, and some parents are reluctant to engage generally. It's difficult so there needs to be some creative thinking around it. But it's so important that there is that level of engagement. The more engaged parents are in this topic the best outcomes there are for children.
>
> (Will Gardner, ChildNet Chief Executive, July 2018)

Parents may be surprised, but the evidence also shows that children are keen for their parents to get involved in learning about e-safety, Gardner says. He points to the study[8] for Safer Internet Day 2018, published by the UK Safer Internet Centre, where 77% of children said they wanted to be able to call on their parents if they were struggling with something online. "So there is a clear role for parents to play and children want parents to play that role."

One of the most effective ways of engaging with them is to involve their children as active participants. Inviting parents in for a drama or an assembly run by children on a digital safety topic provides an opportunity for them to hear about what children know about the topic and help kick-start the conversation about safe behaviour.

## Parents and modelling behaviour

The way parents and other adults use technology – whether it's being wedded to the phone, checking the laptop for work e-mail or relentlessly documenting family life on Facebook – inevitably has an effect on children. Modelling appropriate behaviour can be a challenge when so much of all of our lives are now dependent on technology.

Parents' own views and experiences naturally also shape their attitude to what is and isn't acceptable. Some parents will insist on strictly rationing access to technology because of their own rules-based upbringing and approach to life. At the other end of the spectrum, one digital expert who works with schools recalls a female parent at one session voicing surprise at the notion that young people perhaps shouldn't be watching X-rated material online with their parents on the basis that "I used to watch porn films with my dad and it didn't do me any harm." Then there are the parents who made their own porn films and everyone has seen them online.

Much more concerning, schools and social workers have reported instances of inappropriate, over-sexualised behaviour in class by children which can be traced back to dad back at home masturbating while watching online porn with the child in the same room.

"Modelling positive behaviour online and leading by example is incredibly important as that's how children learn," says online safety consultant Traci Good. "If we don't model that good behaviour, how can we expect our children to?"

The longer term impact of inappropriate or just thoughtless online behaviour also needs to be flagged up to parents, she adds.

> Whatever our children are doing online, their digital footprint is going to be there forever. And people will judge our children historically by it because the first thing employers are likely to do today when they received an application for a job is to Google the applicant. So if our children are behaving badly online it could hold them back in years to come. Which means that, as parents, we need to model that good behaviour, and hopefully lead our children by example.

Allied to this, sharenting – sharing pictures of children online for the rest of the family to see – is an enjoyable part of life for many parents but it raises some key issues.

Traci Good says:

> We do a lot of work in school around appropriate sharing of images, so if I ask a room full of primary children about the rules for posting pictures of others most will agree that you need permission to post your friend's picture online. If we ask the same group of children if their parents share pictures of them online most will agree that yes, that happens. Ask them if parents ask their permission and the majority of children say that no, parents don't ask their permission. A significant number of children, in my experience, will say their parents have posted pictures that the child wishes they hadn't shared publicly.

She recommends talking to parents about the digital footprint and the fact that today's children will be the most Googled cohort in history so far and everything we share adds to their footprint.

> As parents we need to think critically. Are we inadvertently damaging our children's future by posting pictures of them having a paddy or sharing with the world a video of them going on the potty for the first time ever? It's not just employers and universities that may see this, equally damaging can be the fall-out from friends, which can lead to bullying and social exclusion.

We encourage parents to ask their children if a picture can be shared, and we empower children to feel able to request a picture is removed if they don't feel it is appropriate or even if they simply don't want it sharing.

## Key numbers

Thirty-nine per cent of 8–11 year olds and 83% of 12–15 year olds have their own smartphone

Ninety-nine per cent of 12–15 year olds are online as are half (53%) of 3–4year olds, 79% of 5–7 year olds and 94% of 8–11 year olds.

A tablet is the device most likely to be used by 5–15 year olds to go online.

YouTube is the most recognised content provider among 12–15 year olds, with 94% saying they had heard of it, followed by ITV (89%), Netflix (87%) and BBC One/BBC Two (82%).

Two-thirds of 12–15 year olds say they have a good balance between screen time and doing other things, and a majority of parents agree.

Managing screen time gets more difficult as children get older: 12% of parents of 3–4 year olds agree that they "find it hard to control their child's screen time," increasing to 41% of parents of 12–15 year olds.

A quarter of 8–11 year olds and three-quarters of 12–15 year olds have a profile on a social media or messaging site or app.

Parents are more likely to be aware of the minimum age for Facebook than for Instagram, Snapchat or WhatsApp. It is 13 for all of them.

Two in five parents whose child uses social media or messaging services say they would allow their child to use them before reaching the required minimum age

(*continued*)

## Key numbers (*continued*)

Nearly all parents of 3–4 year olds and 5–15 year olds mediate their child's use of the internet in some way, either technical tools, supervision, rules or talk to child about staying safe online.

More than four in five parents of 5–15 year olds who go online say they have spoken to their child about how to stay safe online and two in five parents of 5–15 year olds say they talk to their child at least every few weeks about how to stay safe online.

A majority of parents of 5–15 year olds agree with this statement "I trust my child to use the internet safely" (81%).

Source: Ofcom's Children's and parents' media use and attitudes report in 2017

## What are parents concerned about?

More than four in ten parents of 5–15 year olds are concerned about companies collecting information about what their child is doing online (46%).

Five aspects are of concern to around four in ten parents of 5–15 year olds who go online: cyberbullying (40%), their child giving out details to inappropriate people (39%), how much time their child spends online (39%), their child seeing content online that encourages them to harm themselves (38%) and their child damaging their reputation (37%).

Around one in three are concerned about the content of the websites their child visits, or the pressure on their child to spend money online (both 35%).

(*continued*)

## What are parents concerned about? (*continued*)

A quarter of parents are concerned about the possibility of their child being radicalised online (25%).

### *Internet matters*

A report produced for Internet Matters pinpointed the typical worries of parents as the following:

- Content – what are children looking at?
- Contact – who are they speaking to?
- Conduct – how do they present themselves and engage with others?

Sources: Ofcom, Internet Matters: *Parenting Digital Natives, Concerns and Solutions*

## Steps parents take

Most parents surveyed by Ofcom in 2017 confirmed they have measures in place to manage their children's media use. They do the following:

- Talk to their children about staying safe online.
- Use technical tools.
- Supervise their child.
- Create rules.

(*continued*)

## Steps parents take (*continued*)

16% of parents of 3–4 year olds who go online and 40% of parents of 5–15 year olds use all four types of approach, and nearly all parents use at least one.

Around four in ten parents of 5–15 year olds use filters on their home broadband.

Source: Ofcom, 2017

## General tips for parents

Teachers and parents need to understand what children are doing online and taking a realistic approach. It's about making sure that the advice they are giving is fresh and up to date. 'Don't talk to strangers online' won't work if children are regular gamers, for example.

But if children do have online gaming friends, make sure they know they should not personal and private information with them if they haven't met in real life. Be clear: keep your in-gaming friends very firmly in-game.

As one e-safety specialist says, most children have seen something inappropriate online and they fear that, "if their parents or teachers knew they'd seen it, they would be in trouble – even though it's often something they have stumbled across and they are not purposely looking for it." A good tip for parents is that when your child tells you about something that they have seen online that has scared them or worried them, don't take away their device as a kneejerk reaction, because the next time they see something they won't tell you. The lines of communication need to be open, so have a conversation with them. Parents might be

(*continued*)

## General tips for parents (*continued*)

alarmed that their child has seen something horrific or upsetting, but it's far more important to have the conversation about what it is they have seen and how to make sure that it doesn't happen again, so the child knows the parent is a safe place to come to. Scare stories seldom work, so trying to scare children into behaving differently can be counterproductive.

Children aren't going to stop going online so the best thing we can do is educate them, be interested in what our children are doing and be there for them and be approachable so that your child knows that if anything happens, that they can come to you.

Don't be wedded to your phone at the school gate. Some schools put up signs to this effect.

We encourage parents to ask their children if a picture can be shared, and we empower children to feel able to request a picture is removed if they don't feel it is appropriate (or even if they simply don't want it shared).

## Family agreement sheet

A family agreement sheet or contract sets out what rules parents and children agree they will abide for online. It can be done as a homework exercise so children go home and talk to their parents about what the rules are in school, what they rules are at home and how they might be different.

It can cover elements such as these:

- How long children should spend online each day or each week?
- Should more time be allowed at the weekend?

(*continued*)

## Family agreement sheet (*continued*)

- Are children allowed to download an app without their parents' permission?
- Should there be different rules for younger children and older siblings?

There is more information for parents at www.saferinternet.org.uk/advice-centre/parents-and-carers/resources-parents-and-carers including a link to Childnet's family agreement www.childnet.com/resources/family-agreement

## Case study: Digital picnic

At King's Ely Junior School in Cambridgeshire, staff have run digital picnics, inviting parents into school for a combined social and technology session starting at 4.30pm and running for an hour.

They are led by the school's digital leaders – trained students from Years 6 and 7 – who created a set of resources to explain to parents how popular apps and games such as Fortnite work. There are separate events for parents of Years 6–8 and for Years 3–5 focussing on slightly different material.

At the picnic, tables are set up where groups of children showed how they used the technologies so their parents could see them in action and ask questions. Parents are routinely surprised at the level of their children's knowledge and the skill and dexterity they display at gaming.

Parents and their children sit around clusters of tables in the hall. Staff give a short talk on how digital safety is taught in school in lessons and in form time.

(*continued*)

## Case study: Digital picnic (*continued*)

The parental agreement and how to get the balance right in terms of allowing children access to the technologies they love but preventing the excessive use which parents worry about is also covered here.

Following the talk, parents are able to wander around 'the stalls' with their children talking to the digital leaders, and to the staff, and taking some of the printed material the children had produced for them.

Finally, they sit with their families with sandwiches and drinks at the tables to discuss the different games and apps they have learnt about. They also look at the family agreement.

A key message the school wanted to convey to parents was to avoid imposing a ban on a game or app because children will easily find a way to circumvent it by going to a friend's house or using free WiFi elsewhere. Instead, the focus was on behaviour and helping parents to help their children use their devices safely.

With the contract, parents were encouraged to explain why they want to limit children's online time so the children understand that there is a rationale and not a blanket rule. But, equally, it provides an opportunity for children to explain why they love a particular game and what they get out of and make their case for having more time to play. The theory is that ff parent and child understand each other's position, then they should be able to find a compromise which satisfies concerned parent and keen gamer.

The picnic worked because it was largely led by the children and wasn't the standard lecture from staff on dos and don'ts of technology, says Daniel Everest, the school's head of computing and digital innovation.

"The face-to-face event has a greater impact than parents going online and watching videos and the fact that they are learning about what their children know is very appealing," he says.

(*continued*)

## Case study: Digital picnic (*continued*)

"Parents are routinely surprised at the level of their children's knowledge and, sometimes, they can be shocked that their children have a level of skill and are posting pictures and comments online about things their parents know nothing about, so it's quite eye-opening for them."

Steve Farmer, a parent at the school who has a tech background and is on the school's digital safety committee, agrees there is a degree of naivety among some adults about what their children can do online and how the nature of social interaction has changed.

> In the end, the best thing that parents can do to keep kids safe online is keep talking to them. Online, children can talk to people you have never met all the time and, as a parent, while you can try to turn the broadband off at home, that won't stop them going elsewhere to use the internet. Things like the digital picnic are really effective because the children are teaching their parents but also because they encourage communication about these topics.
>
> (Daniel Everest, head of computing and innovation, King's Ely Junior School, Cambridgeshire, July 2018; Steve Farmer, parent, King's Ely Junior School, Cambridgeshire, August 2018)

## Case study: iVengers

In Derbyshire, the iVengers scheme is doing exactly that. Funded by Derbyshire Police and Crime Commissioner, the project with Years 5 and 6 pupils at schools in Chesterfield is aimed at preventing problems with online safety by involving parents and children in learning.

(*continued*)

## Case study: iVengers (*continued*)

It supports Ofsted requirements and statutory guidance, *Keeping Children Safe in Education (2018)* but, importantly, links children's behaviour in the classroom to their online behaviour at home.

It features a monthly task in which children create a resource to help develop everyone's understanding of an online safety issue.

For example, one month the children made a three-minute video clip that explored the pros and cons of the online game Fortnite, which was hugely popular with children but was disliked by some parents because it revolved around shooting.

The children wrote a script, considering first how they might persuade their parents to let them play the game.

Traci Good, who is leading the project, says we need to focus on the benefits – not just the negative aspects – of being online so parents fully understand their children's experience.

"That way, they can talk about teamwork, good hand-eye co-ordination and planning skills and also being allowed to communicate with friends," she says.

Children who didn't live with one of their parents may also have seen the game as a way of connecting with that parent, and so viewed it positively for other reasons besides entertainment, she adds.

The children then played devil's advocate and wrote the other half of the script from a parent's perspective, considering why a parent might object to them playing the game and how parental controls might be employed to limit their playing.

> Children are very quick on this. They know that their parents might object because the game has guns and it features the floss dance as a way of celebrating when a player has killed someone which a parent might think is not OK.
>
> But children also know how the parental controls work, which parents might not, so that's useful knowledge that they can share with them in this video.

(*continued*)

## Case study: iVengers (*continued*)

Once the monthly video is made, the school can send the link out via text or other message – so parents are not obliged to come into school – and it is also hosted on the school's website.

"We use it as a piece of persuasive writing for children and they buy into *it* because they are writing about a game and it means they can make a YouTube video," Traci says.

Having watched the video, parents can assess the benefits and risks of the game and then make a choice about whether they are happy for their child to continue playing it.

The project was led by young people as parents are far more likely to engage with the work if their children are leading it, Traci says.

"We know that by putting on an event in a school hall and saying 'come to our event' some parents might turn up but not necessarily the ones that we need to get."

## Case study: Online gaming (anonymous)

Learning about e-safety can teach children and parents many things, including the value of money – or, in the case of one parent, the value of virtual money.

"A parent came to see us after he received a large credit card bill," recalls a teacher at one primary school where e-safety is embedded across the curriculum and which works closely with parents.

> He had no idea what it was for but he knew it was something technological that his child had done and wanted to find out what to do. What had happened was that the child

(*continued*)

### Case study: Online gaming (anonymous) (*continued*)

> had played something very popular called Roblox, one of the big, child-centred games, which is about building things and you can put extra money in to get extra materials. The parent had left all of his credit card details loaded into the game. The child, who didn't understand that the 'virtual currency' he was playing with was actually real money, was having a great time, buying this and that and racked up a huge bill. The parent didn't notice until it was taken out of his account.

The parent was angry about the incident, though not at his son.

> He came to us and asked for help on how to approach it. First we had a look at CommonSense Media, read the reviews for the game and did some teaching about what online currency or virtual currency is and how you can prevent things like this happening. But we also talked about the kind of language you can use with a child when a mistake does happen – saying to the child 'I think you've made a poor choice, rather than you been naughty.' We also talked about how to explain what the child could and couldn't do on the game in future so it didn't appear as an arbitrary ban – which the child might have circumvented anyway in the future. All of this advice is rooted in a values system where the pupil is clear any steps taken are because the parents and school care.

"That is what's important with any of these issues," he adds. "E-safety can seem quite nebulous but we always relate it to values which means we have a universal language with children when something goes wrong so we can demonstrate respect and consistency with both pupils and parents."

## Case study: The White Horse Federation, Swindon

James Summerson, the lead for online safety for the White Horse Federation in Swindon, supports primary schools in developing online safety in the curriculum. Schools in the federation are encouraged to aim for the QA Mark in online safety, an award which indicates that policy, leadership, technical infrastructure, staff training, community work and the curriculum are all geared to achieving a deep understanding of safety issues.

Working with parents, many of whom are aware that online safety for their children is a concern, the schools' work allows the children to achieve a fuller understanding of and engagement with the issues of online safety. James says the following:

> Media coverage has helped to flag this up but the concern tends to be quite reactive in the sense that parents are worried about the latest app or about the idea that if the kids go online, they are going to get contacted by someone who has nefarious intentions towards them this informs the kind of responses that they see as being effective. It's also very much characterised as a technological problem that must have a technological solution.
>
> For example, 'If I lock the phone down, supervise the children 24 hours a day, it's going to be safe,' whereas the message we are trying to promote is about safe behaviour all the time and students making the right choices. More often than not, you tend to find that the children who are forbidden from going online at home will go round to a friend's or find an unsecured WiFi and look at all the things parents don't want them to see.
>
> (James Summerson, lead for online safety, White Horse Federation, Swindon, July 2018)

(*continued*)

## Case study: The White Horse Federation, Swindon (*continued*)

Pegi, the Europe-wide game rating system, reports that one of the major issues is children playing games that are rated 18.

James agrees:

> The children are playing those at seven, eight and nine years old and the parents really don't have an understanding of what's on a particular game. There's a perception that because it's a computer game and not a film, it doesn't have the same impact or content as an 18-rated film would. But an 18-rated game means there is usually very unsuitable content.
>
> There's also a lack of understanding about how interactive games are now – with headsets, consoles and the like – and this is exacerbated by social media and young people wanting to film themselves for YouTube playing games. Youngsters are going into a mixed economy in terms of who the users are that they're communicating with at the other end and so often parents don't really appreciate this.

James and the staff will signpost parents to places like Common-Sense Media, which provides ratings for games in terms of what the game entails and an appropriate age level for the game. Importantly these ratings come from two camps – from parents and from children.

> I think parents certainly feel intimidated that they are not the tech experts and it is the young people, from an increasingly young age, that are. The children are always going to be better at using the device than a parent. We rebalance that by reminding parents they have got a better level of judgment, of life experience, so they able to make more informed choices about what children are doing.

(*continued*)

## Case study: The White Horse Federation, Swindon (*continued*)

The schools uses a variety of channels to bring parents on board, though it finds convening school-parent meetings to be the least effective.

> A range of approaches are needed nowadays because we find the traditional face-to-face, after school briefing with staff answering questions at the end has a pretty low impact. Everyone has such busy lives nowadays that not everyone can commit to the time after school. They are still useful – as parents will always talk to each other beyond these meetings – but are part of a raft of techniques we use to get the message out to as many parents as possible.

The federation does use social media to promote online safety messages, particularly Twitter but also Facebook.

"We use Twitter to push out content to parents and we've seen a good response to that," James says.

> For example, when it's Safer Internet Day – which is something all of our schools sign up to – the children create the content themselves around it and an online link to the work they've done will be tweeted. The immediacy of Twitter is useful and followers can be tracked easily. In a school that has really effective practice, parents will re-tweet so the message is spread in yet another way. This variety of channels also include Facebook. The most important thing is to go with what the school community feels comfortable with and what they are already happy with using. Sometimes, when immediacy is of the essence – to alert parents if there's a game we're concerned about, for example – we will use our

(*continued*)

**Case study: The White Horse Federation, Swindon (*continued*)**

> text-to-parent service because it's short and punchy. We all know from our own school days that letters given out to pupils so often remain at the bottom of school bags!

The most effective approach of all, though, is using the children themselves as educators.

> It is always a great, great way to get message out and increase engagement. Schools have days where parents and children come together and learn in the classroom, sharing the journey to a joint understanding. Parents want to see what's happening in the school and what their children are learning but doing it this way takes away some of the 'it's going to be done to you, rather than with you' feel. Parents are keen to understand but it can be quite intimidating to acknowledge they don't have all the answers so this approach addresses that.

## Online safety resources

UK Safer Internet Centre – its role covers a huge array of advice and support for teachers and other professionals who work with children and young people and for parents. One of its key functions is coordinating UK activity for Safer Internet Day in the UK, the annual, global event promoting the safe use of digital technology for children and young people, www.saferinternet.org.uk. There is also a dedicated section on social media www.saferinternet.org.uk/advice-centre/social-media-guides

EPICT – the European Pedagogical ICT Licence, a qualification for schools in online safety www.epict.co.uk/

360 Safe – a free online tool to help schools review online safety policy and practice https://360safe.org.uk/

ChildNet International – the online safety charity carries out research and provides free resources for schools and families to help them get to grips with digital safety issues, www.childnet.com/

NSPCC – the charity's work on online safety encompasses children, families and teachers, including staff training, ideas for lessons and policy. Its Net Aware tool, developed with O2, provides a guide to popular apps and games and the Net Aware website contains case studies on parents' young people's experiences and online-safety information. www.nspcc.org.uk/services-and-resources/research-and-resources

Other sites recommended by teachers and parents featured in this chapter include:

ParentZone – advice aimed at parents, https://parentzone.org.uk/

Internet Matters – another parent-facing organisation, backed by industry, www.internetmatters.org/

Common Sense Media – a site for parents, teachers and young people with advice and tools to help navigate the online world, www.commonsensemedia.org

ChildLine and the ForMe app, which children can use to text a Childline counsellor who can text them back, www.childline.org.uk/toolbox/for-me

JN

## Notes

1 Children and Parents: Media Use and Attitudes Report, Ofcom, 2017.
2 Children and Parents: Media Use and Attitudes Report, Ofcom, 2017.
3 BESA annual ICT research report, 2017.
4 The British Educational Suppliers Association (BESA), 2017.
5 Letting Children Be Children, Report of an Independent Review of the Commercialisation and Sexualisation of Childhood by Reg Bailey, 2011.
6 Garmendia, Garitaonandia, Martinez, & Casado, 2012; Livingstone, 2013.
7 Livingstone, S., Ólafsson, K., Helsper, E. J., Lupiáñez-Villanueva, F., Veltri, G. A., and Folkvord, F. (2017) Maximizing opportunities and minimizing risks for children online: The role of digital skills in emerging strategies of parental mediation, *Journal of Communication*, 67(1) (1 February), 82–105, https://doi.org/10.1111/jcom.12277
8 Digital Friendships: the role of technology in young people's relationships.

# 4 Raising aspirations

## Introduction

Social mobility – the ability of a person to rise through the socio-economic levels based on talent, hard work and application, rather than class or wealth – has been a key topic in education for at least 20 years. Successive governments have tried to address it with initiatives such as the Unlocking Talent, Fulfilling Potential strategy of 2017, as have charities such as the Sutton Trust and Achievement for All.

The barriers to social mobility and the reasons for them are complex, but it boils down to this: talent is spread evenly across this country but opportunity is not and social class remains the strongest predictor of achievement in school.[1] If you grow up in a poor home, your chances not just of gaining access to the jobs and life chances but of realising your potential are lower than those of children growing up in middle-class households. The Sutton Trust Social Mobility report in 2010[2] found that by the time they are five, children growing up in the poorest fifth of families were already nearly a year behind their peers from middle-income families in vocabulary tests and the gap only widens as the children grow up. Parenting and the home learning environment were the key influences that accounted for half of the 11-month development gap at age five, the report concluded.

When it comes to higher education, the number of young people from disadvantaged backgrounds going to 'elite' universities rose slightly in 2016–2017, though from a very low base: UCAS data for

2006–2017[3] showed that entry rates for 18 year olds to the higher tariff HE institutions rose from 2.3% to 4% for those from areas of England where numbers going to university are historically the lowest (as defined by the POLAR system which classifies local areas into five groups, based on the proportion of 18 year olds who enter HE aged 18 or 19 years old). But the numbers are still far below the national average and, once at university, those from disadvantaged backgrounds are also more likely to drop out in their first year.[4]

Parents play a crucial role in supporting children's learning, experts agree,[5] and familial attitudes are deeply influential when it comes to shaping children's attitudes and ambitions. Does this mean that poorer families are more likely to put their children off university? Of course not. But what it does indicate is that these parents are likely to find it harder to know how to support their children to help them get there – "Every parent wants to do the best for their child. But for those parents who have the money, it is easier than for others," as Sutton Trust founder Sir Peter Lampl sums it up.[6]

Meanwhile, the Educational Endowment Foundation, which analyses the impact of scores of learning initiatives, included ones aimed at improving parental engagement, highlighting that low participation and retention rates are often major stumbling blocks when it comes to successfully translating a desire for parental involvement into reality.

This chapter looks at some of the factors which affect aspiration specifically and at ways in which schools can work with parents, both from disadvantaged backgrounds but also from high-achieving ones, to the opportunities their children have in today's world. It looks at a scheme to encourage young people into the elite set of Russell Group universities who may not have considered applying otherwise and at a school where inclusion strategy included a focus on engaging parents in order to raise aspirations across a community.

## Background: what do we mean by 'disadvantage'?

The factors which deter young people from aiming high are complex but include the following:

- No one in the family has ever been to or applied to a top university.
- The child doesn't know anyone in the wider family community who has done so.
- Fear of fees and lack of understanding about how the system works.
- The posh tag of 'elite' universities.
- Media coverage of the lack of diversity at elite institutions.

For any individual pupil, those factors could be multiple: it could come down to one particular thing that is of utmost importance to them. But it's a persistent problem that even though different governments have tried to target in different ways, it appears that it persists in society and young people from these particular backgrounds are unable to conceive of themselves as fitting in and belonging in these elite universities.

### Case study: ROAR programme

The ROAR programme at St Edmund Arrowsmith RC High School, a voluntary-aided 11–16 school with around 1,200 pupils in Wigan, has run for three years.

ROAR – it stands for Russell Group or Alternative Ready – encourages pupils to aim 'as high as possible' by nurturing an environment of aspiration and excellence from the day the students join the school in Year 7. The first cohort took their A levels in summer 2018. Louise Payne, associate assistant head, who coordinates the programme, says the focus is on encouraging young people to think 'Why not me?'

"We want to introduce them to the idea of the Russell Group universities, that there is some real quality provision out there and so why shouldn't you, as a Northern working-class person, put

(*continued*)

## Case study: ROAR programme (*continued*)

yourself forward for a place at one of them. Why shouldn't you be aspiring to be among the intellectual elite?"

The programme is launched with an assembly to pupils from different year groups ranging from Year 7 to 10 where they are introduced to some of the Russell Group universities and what they offer and how going to one may help the students fulfil life and career ambitions. Concepts such as 'growth mindset' and the values of hard work and determination are emphasised as essential for any student who sets their sights on a place there.

There is competition for places – just 20 per programme – and students complete a short application with a recommendation from someone outside the school, plus a personal statement of why they want to pursue the programme and details of progress in their subjects and extra-curricular activities. If they are successful, they are informed through an official letter in the post. Unsuccessful students can reapply for the next round.

The staff identify a big theme, normally based around philosophical concepts or a current issue of global or national significance, such as how the world's cyber-journey will progress over the next 50 years or to what extent is the north/south divide a reality in 21st-century Britain? The pupils then begin a research-based task centred on the question and have additional sessions on research skills, building resilience and critical thinking. At the end, the projects are presented to fellow students, staff and parents and students 'graduate,' receiving a first, second or third class grade for their dissertations. By the end of their school career, regular participants will have made four or five visits to different Russell Group universities, including one to either Oxford or Cambridge.

Parents are encouraged to help children with the application and getting a reference from a non-family member, and, if their

(*continued*)

## Case study: ROAR programme (*continued*)

child is successful, are invited into school to a presentation by someone from a Russell Group University to hear about the work involved.

These parental meetings are key to the success of the project; rather than a transmission of information from school to parent, they are pitched as a coming together of professionals and families so that the children hear the same messages about ambition, hard work and application at home and in school. Parents have the contact details for the key staff on the ROAR programme organisers so that they can ask questions and get updates on how their child is progressing at any time during the programme. They also receive postcards giving quantitative and qualitative information about their child's progress over the year.

"The launch is an informal gathering so that parents feel they aren't being talked at," Louise Payne says.

> We talk generally about the benefits of a university education – some or our parents have studied at university and some haven't – and about what the Russell Group universities are and why we encourage children to set their sights on one. Part of it is about nurturing that sense that our children are as entitled as any to see themselves as heading for the best that society can offer them. One year, for example, I talked about Prince George who had just started school. A radio presenter had mentioned that even at the age of four, the children in Prince George's school shook hands with their class teacher because such behaviour would be expected of the pupils who might one day become future leaders. To me, that firm handshake symbolised everything that children of a particular background are imbued with from a young age and I made the point to our parents that there's no reason

(*continued*)

## Case study: ROAR programme (*continued*)

> why our children shouldn't have the same confidence and belief in themselves, why they shouldn't be aspiring to be the leaders of the future in their fields by going to a top university. We say to parents "We are a good school, our students get excellent results, so the world is their oyster."
>
> (Louise Payne, Associate Assistant Head, St Edmund Arrowsmith RC High School, July 2018)

The programme's founder, Phil Denton, was inspired by a personal passion to open doors to the country's elite universities for the children in the school. He wanted to develop ambition and self-belief in the students, encouraging but not pressuring them to aim high and fulfil their potential and to nurture that belief, too, in their parents and teachers.

Phil, now head at St Bede's Catholic High School in Ormskirk, says the element of competition was one of the things that drew parents in in the beginning though some also had reservations about the scale of the task their children were undertaking.

> At that first meeting, we had a lot of questions from parents who were concerned we might be putting pressure on the children, which I was quite surprised about. They were worried that the children wouldn't have the ability to be able to write and think in the academic style and at the level we aiming for and that it would be too much extra work. But they were reassured when we said we were confident that, with support, the pupils would be up to it and that we would also give them the time to do their projects, rather than it be extra work.
>
> The way that I pitched it to parents was, they are going to be sitting with their friends, doing activities that are enjoyable and at the end of it they will get feedback. They will

(*continued*)

## Case study: ROAR programme (*continued*)

> leave with a positive sense of what going to university is and what the opportunities are but we also stressed that it gave the kids the opportunity to aim for a Russell Group University ultimately but that, if they decided not go to, it didn't render them a failure.
>
> (Phil Denton, Head, St Bede's Catholic High School, Ormskirk, August 2018)

Parents also had confidence in the structure once it was set out.

> We told them in detail what the kids would be doing each week and that it was about the research nature of Russell Group universities that we were focussing on so their child would be researching a specific topic.
>
> One of the parents said, "My child's no good at researching" so I asked them what the child wanted for Christmas and whether they were any good at researching then or when they were interested in a particular computer game could they research it on the internet. Pupils can use search engines, they can find information, they can make a distinction between two different brands or choices, so that made it something parents knew the children were able to do.

And despite the emphasis on aspiration, it was important to underline to parents that the project wasn't about burnishing the school's reputation by sending a stream of youngsters to Oxbridge but about opening pupils' eyes to the choices available to them, if they wanted and were willing to work for them.

> The difference for me with this programme is it's not about the school imposing the values and aspirations of somebody

(*continued*)

## Case study: ROAR programme (*continued*)

else but about the children exploring themselves and their own abilities. It's not about saying that there's anything wrong with the area they come from so they need to escape it but that there are more opportunities to use the talents they already possess.

## Case study: Flying High Trust

Cotgrave Candleby Lane School is a high-achieving primary in south Nottinghamshire and part of the Flying High Trust.

In 2012, Chris Wheatley, then executive head, instigated a new school improvement strategy. He was concerned that a culture of low aspiration had been tolerated rather than challenged but he knew that the answers lay outside the school, as well as in it.

Cotgrave is a former mining village with higher than average unemployment and with numbers of children who were eligible for free school meals also above the national average. There was a general lack of aspiration within the community; a child interested in cooking was "more likely to set her sights on becoming a waitress than owning her own restaurant," Wheatley recalled at the time. It was compounded by many parents' distrust of 'school' and 'the system' based on their own bad experiences of education, a negative stance some were passing on to their children.

"Parental disengagement was a real problem and the consequence for their children was that they weren't getting the broader access to the curriculum that they needed with parents who would extend what was done in class at home. It meant that the education the child had in school was fragmented."

(*continued*)

## Case study: Flying High Trust (*continued*)

Tackling 'engagement' was about more than putting on after-school clubs "We needed to engage parents so that they could begin to see education as not just a 9–3.30pm thing," he says.

The new strategy focussed on inclusion but in the broadest sense rather than narrowly on children with special needs, aiming to engage all parents more closely in the education of their child as a route to raising not just standards but the child's aspirations for life.

"My view was that it wasn't about 'hard to reach' it was about 'scared to come in,' so we needed to be about breaking down cyclical barriers, usually of parents that had lost trust in the education system because they had lost trust themselves when they were in it. They very much saw schools as an institution and one to be feared rather than having ownership of it."

Candleby made several attempts at putting on activities to draw parents in but had little success at first. "We put on English courses, no one turned up. But one of the best things was breakfast cobs. In the morning when parents were dropping the children off, I'd invite the parents in for breakfast with free breakfast cobs and once they were in, the idea was the teachers would show them what the kids were doing and talk about how parents could support them."

Even with the cob inducement, it was slow to take off.

(Some of this material first appeared in a case study written for the then National College for School Leadership in 2011)

> I did it twice and hardly anyone turned up. So then I went on to the streets outside, peddling them to parents to get them in. I didn't want it to seem like a gimmick and I knew it probably wouldn't work with the parents we really wanted to come in so I decided we'd make it a regular event every

(*continued*)

## Case study: Flying High Trust (*continued*)

half-term – come and have a breakfast cob with us and your children. I got probably 50 the first time and a hundred the next, then 200 and before long it becomes just what happens at the school.

And once we had the 200 in, we could be braver. We got rid of the first hour of the school day and had the parents coming into the classrooms, having a go at a few things, talking to the teachers. It was a drip-drip-drip effect until that kind of engagement becomes part of the culture.

(Chris Wheatley, Chief Executive,
Flying High Trust, August 2018)

Another element of the strategy drew on Achievement for All (AfA) techniques, including close tracking of children's progress in English and maths and a focus on addressing persistent absence or social skills.

Parent forums were convened to explain the Assessment for All project and its philosophy and to gather their ideas as it progressed. In fact, parents who were initially involved became strong advocates for inclusion as the project progressed and their experiences of how they had been helped as a family by it were a powerful support when it came to expanding the scheme to others.

A crucial element was the 'structured conversation' on educational outcomes between teacher and a child's parent. Lasting around 45 minutes and directed mainly by the parent with the teacher as listener, it provided an opportunity for parents to share their concerns about their children, to reflect on the positives and to explain what their hopes are and where they feel they want their child to go. The teacher has a similar mini-structured conversation with the pupil which about what they want to get better at, what could be done in school to help and what could

(*continued*)

## Case study: Flying High Trust (*continued*)

be done at home which would feedback into the conversation with the parents.

Part of the conversation was to agree targets for the child which can be straightforward – progress in reading – or other ones which the parents raise. In one example, the structured conversation with parent and child revealed that one child who was a non-attender and whose progress was poor was effectively the sole carer for a much younger sibling. The school took steps, including arranging for the pupil to bring the other child to the school's breakfast club. Her attendance record was perfect from that day, enabling her to make two years' progress in one year and it remained perfect when she went to secondary school.

In terms of results, the impact of making inclusion a whole-school approach was marked. It helped the school to boost standards across the board and although many pupils arrived with attainment levels below the national average the school's KS2 scores were high. In 2012, 92% of the pupils achieved level 4 in English and maths, compared with a national average of 79% and a local average of 82%. Children on free school meals outperformed their peers and the emphasis on one-to-one parental support had helped the school to find out how to unblock whatever was preventing the child from learning.

Feedback from parents in questionnaires was also highly positive. In interviews with pupils, meanwhile, they can clearly articulate their targets and also explain how things have changed for the better for them at school and at home.

By 2018, the inclusion strategy had paid off to the extent that parental involvement in the school and with their children's learning was accepted as a matter of course. "Our parents know that if their child comes here, the adults are expected to join in the life of the school and get involved in learning. It's the way

(*continued*)

## Case study: Flying High Trust (*continued*)

things are," Wheatley says. "It's almost an unwritten rule that they have to come in and that they know they are going to be involved in their child's education."

The Flying High Trust has grown to 23 schools with Wheatley as chief executive and the aim is to roll out the approaches to parental engagement and the structured conversations to all of the schools.

One thing that has changed since the first years, says Wheatley, is the understanding of the importance of starting the work in early years and working with parents not just when they join the school but even before.

> What I've found now is that actually there is a massive need for early intervention. Primary schools are into intervention all of the time but the earlier you can get the children caught up in the early years, the more effect you are going to have in that progress route, Year 2 to Year 6. One of the main ways to do that catch-up is effective parental engagement. So it isn't just about engaging with all parents, it's also about engaging with the foundation parents effectively and, more really engaging with those parents who are not even foundation yet.

In some of the trust's most challenging communities, it has created links with private nursery providers with teachers from the trust going in to talk not just to the staff, which would be the norm, but to make sure they talk to the parents of the nursery children too by being there at the start and end of the day and form relationships with them before they are even at the school. A lot of the trust schools also have their own two-year-old provision and nurseries on site.

(*continued*)

## Case study: Flying High Trust (*continued*)

"Those schools are now flying because we have got the kids as early as we possibly can and the parental collaboration as early as we possibly can."

Parental engagement needs to go hand-in-hand with support, he adds.

"What you find is that if you engage parents then you need to support them so that they engage even more and it doesn't become a one-off. It's about schools understanding where are the barriers to getting and keeping the parents coming in and engaging to give them that sense of ownership and that they are part of that triangle of parent, teacher and child."

There is now a set of Flying High alumni, a scheme which started at Candleby Lane, with a gallery of aspiration: young people who have risen high after school, whether that is university, in the commercial world or otherwise.

> It's a whole range. We've had our first commercial pilot, a stand-up comedian, an Olympian and one of our former pupils has gone to Harvard. They get their picture in the galleries, what they are doing, what they got from school, what Cotgrave means to them.
>
> The young ones are looking up to this now. They see: this is something that the school does and this is something I want to aspire to. I want my picture on that wall.

## Resources

Achievement for All – the charity works with schools on programmes under specific headings, such as Achieving Early, Achieving Schools and Achieving Wellbeing. https://afaeducation.org/

The Education Endowment Foundation, a charity focussed on breaking the link between family wealth and children's success in education and which gathers detailed evidence on the efficacy of programmes to determine 'what really works.' https://educationendowmentfoundation.org.uk

The Sutton Trust funds numerous research and practical projects to address the barriers to education for children from poor backgrounds. It runs the Parental Engagement Fund, set up in 2015 with a grant from the Esmee Fairbairn Trust, www.suttontrust.com

The Social Mobility Foundation – is a charity which helps bright 16–17 year olds from low income backgrounds to access support and networks which will boost their chances of a top university place www.socialmobility.org.uk

JN

## Notes

1 Becky Francis et al. RSA Identities and Practices of High Achieving Pupils 2011.
2 https://www.suttontrust.com/wp-content/uploads/2010/02/Sutton_Trust_Cognitive_Report-2.pdf
3 Office for Fair Access Annual report, 2017–18, p. 9.
4 https://www.hesa.ac.uk/news/08-03-2018/non-continuation-tables
5 Parental Engagement Fund report – the Sutton Trust, January 2018.
6 Sir Peter Lampl, chair of the Sutton Trust, introduction to Parent Power? Using money and information to boost children's chances of educational success by Professor Becky Francis and Professor Merryn Hutchings.

# 5 Parents' evenings

## Introduction

However much schools recognise the importance of parental engagement, if you ask most teachers what the most stressful thing about their job is, the chances are they will reply that it is meeting parents.

Of all the possible ways of engaging families, parents' evenings are arguably the most intimate and intense. One contributor described it like speed-dating – with both sides having high expectations of the meeting, but with only five minutes for either to make any sort of impression before they move on to someone else.

There is a legal requirement for schools to report to parents and provide at least one opportunity a year for parents to discuss their children's progress with a teacher. Schools can, however, decide what form this should take, and how often. Most will hold a parents' evening at least once a year, sometimes more, as well as sending out written reports.

Dr Janet Goodall, lecturer in education leadership and management at the University of Bath, and a leading authority on parental engagement in education, said that while parents' evenings serve a purpose, they could be done better.

> Anecdotally, it seems that they are not as good as they could be, but few schools have tried anything different. Some schools organise tutors' evenings, when they talk to their child's form tutor, but parents whose children attend secondary schools usually want to speak

> to individual subject teachers because the child's achievements may vary from one area of the curriculum to another.
>
> There is no one right way of staging parents' evenings but in the best cases, these discussions take the form of free-flowing conversations, though they may be hindered by time limits. Some schools offer guidance on that sorts of questions parents might want to ask, for example, about the sort of help they can give at home to support their child.

Parents should also have their own questions prepared if possible.

Goodall believes that teachers are often not aware of how impactful such meetings can be with parents, while most families find them nerve-wracking and just being in a school setting may bring back bad memories of their own school days.

A report[1] co-authored by Goodall and Professor Alma Harris *Engaging Parents in Raising Achievement – Do Parents Know They Matter?* commissioned by the then Department for Children, Schools and Families, makes the following observation:

> Ultimately, of course, the reason for giving information to parents is to engage them with the learning of the student. Even when communication is frequent and timely, it sometimes is not effective if schools use jargon or are unclear about the purpose of the communication and the intended response.
>
> Communication ought to be two-way, should be at the point of need and should provide parents with some guidance on how to use or respond to the information.

Goodall adds: "Unfortunately, parents' evenings are not really covered in initial teacher training, or as part as continuing professional development, and both new entrants and experienced teachers would benefit from some training, regardless of what stage they are in their career."

In a 'toolkit'[2] for teachers outlining the point and purpose of parents' evenings, she suggests that rather than reporting to parents on their children's achievements and progress, parents' evening should be about sharing information, and focussed on a partnership between the school and home in educating the child.

So instead of blinding parents with the science of reporting, tracking and monitoring – information that could be provided in a written report – the meeting would take the form of a discussion. She says: "Teachers in the UK are highly skilled in conversations around learning, so wouldn't parents' evenings be a good place to utilise those skills?"

So, the focus of the discussion would be less focussed on the teachers, but more around the partnership between parents and teachers to support the child's learning.

There is relatively little research about the impact and effectiveness of parents' evenings partly, perhaps, because it has become the norm that it is something that schools just do as a matter of course, and parents attend. At least, the ones who are more engaged and interested in their children's education do. Most teachers will admit that it is often the parents they are most keen to see who are the least likely to turn up.

And this is one of the problems. Disentangling parental involvement from socio-economic factors such as income and qualifications, and a parent's own experience of school, can make it difficult to establish exactly how effective parents' evenings are in reality.

The Commission on Inequality in Education,[3] published in 2017 by the Social Market Foundation and led by Sir Nick Clegg, tried to make some sense of the impact of parental engagement in schools, including parents' evenings, on children's attainment. The study looked at parental engagement per se, without a particular focus on low parental qualifications or income as a cause of disengagement and disinterest.

The Commission found that children who had someone in attendance at their parents' evening had much higher test scores at age 11 and made better progress between the ages of 5 and 11 years. Children whose parents or carers turned up to parents' evenings made 1.26 points better progress between the ages of 5 and 11 than those that did not.

The study found that "children faced an even bigger disadvantage if their parent reported there being no parents' evening at their child's school, with their progress between ages 5 and 11 being 1.88 points lower than those with someone attending a parents' evening."

However, the Commission couldn't be certain why this should be the case.

> It is unclear exactly how to interpret this: it may be the school had no parents' evening, or it may be that the parent was simply unaware of it. We expect that the latter is more likely. Either way this is a significant gap in parental engagement; and one that has a clear impact on test scores.

By examining the academic progress of children involved in the Millennium Cohort Study, the Commission established that attendance at parents' evenings was a strong predictor of higher test scores at the age of 11, while failure to attend led to lower test scores. However, it could not separate this from the evidence that showed that parental income and qualifications also had an impact on how well a child performs – and that this also affected the likelihood that they would attend parents' evenings.

Dimitra Hartas, associate professor at the Centre for Education Studies at the University of Warwick, believes that a failure by mothers or fathers to attend parents' evenings is not necessarily an indicator of their investment in their child's education.

Hartas, who has carried out extensive research into child development, and the involvement of parents in education from a social perspective, says parents' evenings are an important first step in parents getting to know teachers, and vice versa.

"Parents' evenings are a very basic type of involvement. What is more important than whether parents turn up, is the quality of the meeting and what is discussed," she says:

> They are a good starting point, but they should then lead to more meaningful interaction between parents and teachers at the next stage. There may be any number of reasons why parents can't or won't attend a parents' evening but their investment in their child's education, in the form of cultural activities or their conversations

> at home, go beyond what happens in the classroom, which is what teachers want to discuss.
>
> (Dimitra Hertas, Telephone interview, August 30 and September 10, 2018)

Regardless of the social-economic and cultural factors, both schools and parents plough on with this annual ritual often more in hope than expectation. Quite simply, in most schools, no more effective method has been found to replace it.

Leo Winkley, former Headmaster of St Peter's School, York, an independent boarding and school, believes parents' evenings matter:

> It's important for parents to be able to look their child's teachers in the eye, and to get a sense of the person before them. The process reinforces the trust that parents put in teachers to educate and care for their child. This meeting is important in developing that sense of trust.
>
> For teachers, it is an opportunity to demonstrate how diligently they have kept records on pupils, and how well they know them. But they need to remember that parents have come to this meeting to be reassured, but not to be confronted with any shocks or surprises. Serious matters need to have been raised earlier.
>
> Nor should it be about attack and defence. The teachers should feel confident enough to explain how they have arrived at their observations, and to state this is what the child is working on and how this will be done.
>
> I became much better at parents' evenings when I became a parent myself, because I realised what it feels like to have someone sitting in front of you discussing your child. Until then you don't really understand that parents might be less rational and more emotional about what you are telling them, and I am not sure you can empathise to the same degree.
>
> (Leo Winkley, Telephone interview, June 25, 2018)

Some schools are now becoming more inventive about how to involve parents who cannot physically attend meetings and the use of technology helps to sustain links that might otherwise be impossible. At Canford, an independent boarding and day school in Dorset, for example, video conferencing or live streaming is used to facilitate the involvement of parents who might be working away or otherwise unable to attend. In this way, parents have also been able to participate in music events, options meetings and parents' evenings.

The use of technology is also mentioned in a National College of School Leadership report *How to involve hard-to-reach parents: encouraging meaningful parental involvement with schools*[4] which states that "it is possible to harness new technologies for parental communication purposes through the use of school blogs and podcasts, a school website (regularly updated) and online questionnaires and resources in order to reach at a distance those who are unable or unwilling to engage with the school in person."

But for most schools, however, parents' evenings remain a straightforward face-to-face transaction.

## A teacher's perspective – Sarah Owens

In a career spanning 25 years in secondary schools, Sarah Owens has reported to literally thousands of families during parents' evenings. While there is no one model for a successful parents' evening and plenty wrong with this system of liaising with parents and carers, she believes parents' evenings present an ideal opportunity to find out about a child and build relationships.

"This partnership is really important. It is an opportunity to meet them face to face and to have that moment when the penny drops about why a pupil is the way they are," she says. "When you see the child in the context of their home background, you can find out so much about them, and what the problems might be."

She recalls one pupil who posed difficulties for teachers because of her defiant behaviour. The girl arrived at the parents' evening with her mother and a younger brother.

This pupil was difficult to teach and reacted badly to criticism or being told off. During the parents' evening she kept hitting her brother and pushing him off his chair. She was also swearing at the mother and accusing her of not caring, and saying she was a waste of space. It was horrible to witness and presented a very awkward situation for me because this was behaviour I would never tolerate in the classroom.

The ultimate authority here was the parent but she was struggling with these difficult children and their behaviour and had no agency. Eventually I told the girl not to swear at her mother and to leave her brother alone. I found myself co-opted into this family dynamic, but it was clear now why the child tried it on in school.

It is not hard to see why parents' evenings are exhausting for teachers. They are most often held straight after school when the teacher has already done a full day's work and is tired. Likewise, parents might be stopping by straight from work. It is not necessarily the ideal scenario to build healthy relationships. For teachers to then face the prospect of talking about classes of students – possibly over several days – can be overwhelming. "I can remember occasions towards the end of a parents' evening when I had no idea what I was saying any more. It was noisy, busy and there were streams of people waiting around."

Owens found parents often reacted to her subject – modern foreign languages – similarly to how they do to maths.

The first thing they will tell you is that they were rubbish at languages and, on some levels, this immediately puts up a barrier that might not exist in other subjects. You find yourself having to speak to people whose own experience of your subject was negative or damaging, who are there to listen to their child's progress in a subject they didn't like themselves or which wasn't a good experience for them.

Complicated domestic situations can also be a challenge.

Sometimes you have parents turning up who are no longer together, or they might have to be seen separately because their own

> relationships are difficult. This effectively means spending twice the amount of time on this one pupil, having to make separate appointments and making sure both parents get the same story, and that a copy of the child's report is sent to both. Sometimes as a teacher you get caught in the middle of their difficulties, with one parent claiming they didn't know about something because no-one told them.
>
> Occasionally, it is the grandparents or a carer who come to parents' evenings, or a parent who does not speak English. Schools provide interpreters where possible, or sometimes an older sibling translates. In such cases, there can be several layers of complexity.

One might assume that working in a county or suburban school in a relatively affluent area would be easier than in an urban area with a diverse population. Owens stresses this isn't necessarily the case.

> It is often the families in the disadvantaged areas who are more responsive because they value education. In more leafy areas you can get more of a push-back. The family may have a big house and smart car, for example, but they will apprentice their son into the family business as soon as he's old enough.
>
> It becomes quite hard to encourage him to learn French when the approach from the family is that he's never going to go to France because his life has been mapped out, so what's the point. You don't want to upset the parents by saying the wrong thing, but you need to get across that there is value to knowing a language.

Owens is now a teacher-trainer at a university school of education and instructs her students how to go about dealing with families and negotiating the, sometimes, tricky world of parents' evenings:

> I always tell them to remember that every pupil is a precious child to their parent or carer, so you have to be careful of the language you use. It actually becomes much easier when you become a

> parent yourself and you empathise with what the parents are going through.
>
> I also tell them to remember that not all parents have had a good experience of school themselves. For some, merely walking into a school can conjure up bad memories, and they feel intimidated by the whole environment. The language the teacher uses, therefore, is really important. It has to be accessible because as a teacher you have an awful lot of data which they might not understand.
>
> My advice is to talk about the individual child and how happy they are in the subject, and how the parents can help and support them. If the conversation needs to touch upon a difficult issue, such as the fact the child always gives in their homework late, talk to the child about this during the discussion and get the child to acknowledge what you are saying in front of the parents. If the parent then says they didn't know homework was due in on a Tuesday, refer them to their diary where this is recorded. That way the whole family knows know what the expectations are.

Teachers who are recently arrived in a school may experience a parents' evening in their first term, before they have had a chance to get to know the names of their pupils. In such cases, having a pile of exercise books on the desk and asking the child to find theirs can help get out of a tricky situation, as well as getting the dialogue going. It removes the potentially embarrassing spectacle of asking the child or parents who they are because you've forgotten.

Be prepared for surprises. Owens once had an otherwise pleasant, hard-working pupil in class who referred to black children using the N-word. "I imagined what the parents must be like but when they came to see me they seemed perfectly normal, well-spoken people but this was clearly the type of language they used at home. I would not have expected this of them."

For some parents, coming face to face with the teacher is an opportunity to set out their own expectations. Owens recalls a father suggesting she gave a boy 'a clip round the ear' if he misbehaved and having to explain to him why she was not allowed to do this.

"What they are saying in this case is 'do what you need to do to make my child do their work.' They are trying to be helpful and supportive."

Owens believe the dialogue shouldn't be restricted to parents' evenings. Just as a teacher might contact or call on a parent to discuss a problem, it is sometimes a good idea to call parents to inform them their child has worked hard and had a good day at school, or to put a note in their homework diary.

"This could have pay-back later when you need to get the parents on-side if something hasn't gone to plan. By acknowledging hard work and effort you are banking good-will for a future time when you might need their help."

## Top tips for a successful parents' evening

- Alert parents to the date of the parents' evening well in advance, so they can organise their time, sort out childcare and make any other arrangements that will enable them to attend.
- Be flexible about the time. If they can only do day-time because of shift work, then try to accommodate them.
- Organise child-care at the school for parents who have nowhere to leave siblings. In primary schools, an empty classroom supervised by a teacher or teaching assistant could be a drop-off point for parents with small children.
- Ensure any serious issues with a child are dealt with earlier. A parents' evening is not the time to discuss specific issues.
- With large cohorts of pupils, consider spacing parents' evenings over more than one day to ensure every parent has enough time to discuss their child.
- Ensure there are senior members of staff close to hand to diffuse potential heated moments.
- Ensure you have the right data about that child in front of you and that you are not telling the parents about another student.

- Don't patronise parents, or blind them with science and the current education-speak. Explain their child's progress in language that they can understand.
- Listen to what parents have to say and follow up their concerns. This might mean referring a situation to senior colleagues.
- If the meeting becomes heated, indicate to a senior member of staff that you need their intervention. This might mean standing up, or any other signal agreed in advance.
- Be respectful. If you're using a lap-top to show data, make sure you look the parents in the eye even though that laptop and its contents might make you feel secure. Remember that not all parents want to know statistics.
- If it's a new year or school, have a crib sheet under the desk with children's names and faces.
- Be welcoming. Stand up to greet parents as they approach and look happy to see them. When their five minutes is up stand up to be clear you, and they, need to move on.
- Say something personal about their children to show you know them and who they are, even if it's only about where they sit in the class or who their best friend is.
- You may have an idea in advance what the parents are like from the conduct and demeanour of the child, but be prepared for surprises.
- Most parents' evenings are quite public events and held in the hall. If you need to talk to them about something sensitive suggest making a separate appointment.
- If the parents or carers don't speak English, try to ensure there is an interpreter present who is not the pupil you are discussing.
- If parents can't attend a parents' evening try to make separate arrangements, or e-mail or call them to discuss their child.
- Consider providing refreshments such as tea and coffee, and biscuits. Parents' evenings are often held when everyone is tired and hungry, and a little hospitality might be welcome and a good icebreaker for conversation.

## A parents' perspective: Eileen Prior, executive director of the Scottish-based charity, Connect, which is dedicated to improving parental engagement in schools

Eileen Prior described parents' evenings as 'a bit like speed-dating.' With their five- or ten-minute slots of movement from one teacher to another, they can be a daunting and uncomfortable experience for parents.

> It seems to be the same the whole country over. These events tend to be chaotic, and are highly pressured situation for teachers, who often won't get to see the parents they most need to talk to.
>
> There must be better ways of managing the flow of information between the school and home, that is more positive, informative and constructive.
>
> (Eileen Prior, Telephone interview, July 20, 2018)

Prior recalls a parents' evening she attended with her son's teachers as illustrative of the many things that are wrong with them. One of his teachers told her that her son's performance would be better if he wasn't constantly absent.

"I was completely thrown by this as he didn't miss school but when I inquired later it turned out that she was referring to days that he represented the school at rugby," Prior said.

> The teacher was saying he was not in lessons and marking him as absent.
>
> This felt to me like a teacher being precious about her subject with little or no understanding that students are real people, who excel at and are interested in other things apart from her lessons.
>
> It was a failure to see the young person's life and their personal development in the context of my son's learning and progress in school.

As the executive director of an organisation seeking to improve the engagement of parents in school, Prior said she wanted to see more initiative and innovation in how parents' evenings could be a better experience all round.

> We seem to be stuck in a rut where we have parents' evenings because this is what we have always done, and not because they are particularly effective. The experience is often unsatisfactory, and parents don't get enough time for a proper dialogue or to find out what they need to know.
>
> They get shown some data and some good work the child has done, and that's it. Your time is up.
>
> It should be about the learning experience and less focus on results, behaviour and the reporting back of data. Not enough of what is discussed is about learning or finding out about the child. How do they live and in what conditions? What are their home circumstances and how is that affecting their learning; how are they coping with adolescence; do they have any worries or fears that might be impacting on their ability to learn?

Prior adds that there is little opportunity for teaches to learn about the interests, hobbies and out-of-school activities that students take part in, and which are important to their development. But even if this information was gathered in the form of a questionnaire, for example, consideration would have to be given on how this information is used and to what effect.

> The situation is slightly easier in primary schools because there are opportunities to see and talk to parents on a daily basis at school drop-off and pick-up times. It becomes more difficult in secondary school when parents are less involved and less engaged. So, we do need a means of schools and families keeping up a dialogue, but I am not convinced that parents' evenings, in their current form, are the answer.
>
> I know teachers who approach parents' evenings with utter dread. There will always be those parents who turn up, in particular those who are keeping a close eye on what is going on with their child's education and who can be quite demanding and vocal

> about what their expectations are, and the information they want to receive about their children's progress.
>
> But the ones the teachers really need to see often don't turn up.
>
> Some parents undoubtedly enjoy parents' evenings because they are socially equipped to deal with that environment. They will go in focused and prepared with questions about the issues that concern them. And they will know they have little cause for concern or to expect to hear something negative as they already have an idea of how well their children is achieving.
>
> But for many parents it is an uncomfortable experience, because their own experience of school wasn't a positive one, or they just feel overwhelmed by the whole experience and lack confidence themselves. They might feel they don't have anything to bring to the table, or to add to the dialogue.

This is where a teacher's skills in imparting the appropriate information and trying to engage and motivate the parents come to the fore.

One of the challenges with parents' evenings, Prior believes, is the mismatch in expectations between what teachers want to discuss and what parents want to know.

> If you ask parents what they want from a parents' evening it is often to find out about the social and emotional aspects of their child's development in the context of the learning process.
>
> They might, for example, want to find out how sociable their son or daughter is; do they get on with other children and have lots of friends; are they happy; do they engage in lessons and contribute to class discussion?
>
> Attainment is often well down the list of things that they want to know about, though it obviously becomes more important as they move through school. Mainly, they want to know that their child is happy.
>
> Instead, schools turn parents' evenings into a discussion on what we can measure and what the outcomes are of that measuring. This is not necessarily the fault of the teachers and is down to pressures associated with school accountability.

The young person needs to be part of this discussion. They need to know what is being said about them and to be part of the dialogue on how they take ownership of their learning. They should not be kept out of the loop of a conversation that is about them.

### Case study: Stanley Park High School, Carshalton

David Taylor describes Stanley Park High School as a 'basket case' when he became head teacher in 2005. He had arrived six years earlier as deputy head, after the school was merged with a nearby failing secondary and with a poor reputation in an area which was highly selective. In the intervening years, little progress had been made in turning the school around.

In the early 2000s pupil results were low at the school, which is based in Carshalton, Surrey, with just 15% of pupils achieving five or more A* to C grades, including English and maths in 2005. "The perception among many parents was 'over my dead body' were they going to send their children here," Taylor says.

> The attitude was "anywhere but Stanley Park". We were perceived as a school for children with special needs, a combination of learning difficulties and behaviour problems.
>
> It would be easy to blame the selective system creaming off the top ability pupils, but that wasn't entirely the cause of our difficulties. The school needed a re-think on how to do things differently for its intake, as we effectively had a grammar school curriculum for all students, with pupils sitting in rows, and this wasn't necessarily appropriate. Added to all this, staff morale and confidence were low.
>
> (David Taylor, Stanley Park School, April 19, 2018)

(*continued*)

## Case study: Stanley Park High School, Carshalton (*continued*)

In 2006, a year after his appointment as head, Taylor was told by the London Borough of Sutton education authority that the school was to be a pathfinder. It was to be a turning point for the school, giving him more freedom to be innovative. "It was the opportunity we needed to re-imagine education and we went off on a bit of a journey," he says. "Literally."

Taylor took himself, and his staff, on a tour of schools that were using inspirational teaching and learning methods and none more so than what he saw in the United States, Iceland and Denmark. He says his eyes were opened around curriculum flexibility and giving students a choice.

"If we were going to re-design the school, we had to focus on aspects such as relationships and not just examination results," Taylor says. "Relationships had been quite poor, and I had to bring parents on side."

> When I started here, it felt like lots of parents didn't want to come into school, or if they did it was because they felt their child had been wronged in some way. It was clear this was going to be complex – we had to consider the relationships between the school and the parents, the parents with their children, and the children with the teachers.
>
> We didn't want to damage relations with the pupils by improving them with the parents. You have to consider the whole. From our perspective we wanted the parents to be involved with their children's education, and in particular the learning side.

One of the ways in which this was achieved was by moving away from the idea of having one parents' evening a year when parents came in to meet the teachers.

(*continued*)

## Case study: Stanley Park High School, Carshalton (*continued*)

> They felt pointless in many ways, and no matter where you put them in the school year, or on what date or time, parents said they were too early or too late, or at that they knew all that about their child already. Parents felt they were getting whole raft of information that was completely useless. We looked at changing that.

Staff at Stanley Park designed what the school calls its Excellent Futures Curriculum (EFC), which took the best part of the national curriculum and, in consultation with businesses, identified the skills young people needed for success at GCSE and beyond. English, maths, science, PE, French and performing arts are still taught separately, but at Years 7 and 8, other subjects are taught in a cross-curricular way under EFC, through project-based learning.

"Every outcome in EFC involves some sort of performance or exhibition that the parents are expected to come and see," Taylor says.

> They are also invited to critique the work and re-draft what they think could be done better. We give them stickers and they can make suggestions, not just with their own child's work but everyone's. This gets the parents used to thinking about their children's learning. We do this about four times during the school year.
>
> Under one topic, called the Sky's the Limit, students will learn how to produce a play – writing a script, making costumes or scenery, about sound and lighting, marketing and directing – rather than just doing drama. The parents are invited in to watch a play written by one of the pupils.

(*continued*)

## Case study: Stanley Park High School, Carshalton (*continued*)

The school then turned its attention to what to do about parents' evenings, in particular in Years 7 and 8. "We thought the current approach of parents making appointments to speak to ten or more teachers wasn't fit for purpose any longer and outdated," Taylor says.

> It didn't seem like an effective means of showing learning to parents.
>
> Students were often not present or felt on the periphery of the process, while the parents felt as judged as their child. We did a survey of parents and it was clear they weren't popular, and turn-out was only just over 50%, so very poor.
>
> There had to be a different way and we believed the child had to be at the centre of the process. Otherwise, we were relying on the parent going home to articulate what had been said, with no guarantee that anything would improve and possibly causing damage to their relationship.

The idea for 'student-led conferences' came from a visit to a school in San Diego, California. At Stanley Park, they take place every February and July, and instead of teachers showing parents a colour-coded spreadsheet or grades and talking generally about the child, it is the students who present their work to the parents.

"They will plan in advance with their tutor what they want to talk about and what pieces of work they want to show," Taylor explains. "It might be something they're particularly proud of, or it might be their worst piece of work, or something they found challenging."

> The pupils have half an hour to present to their parents, and will prepare for it with role play, with the students playing the

(*continued*)

## Case study: Stanley Park High School, Carshalton (*continued*)

part of the parents to they get used to presenting and being questioned.

We also explain to the parents how they should conduct themselves during the conference. If the child is showing them a piece of work we ask them not to criticise their presentation but to suggest questions they might want to ask. It is a very holistic approach.

The preparation for this takes time if you're going to do it properly, and this is why we are at odds with government expectations on accountability. The pupils are not being judged but are presenting to their parents. We consider this to be an important skill, regardless of the fact it cannot be measured in league tables.

Stanley Park tries to be as accommodating as possible so that parents can find a time to attend that suits them. The week before the February half-term, for example, parents have from Wednesday afternoon until Friday lunchtime to attend their child's student-led conference and may ask to be seen up to 10pm.

"For teachers is means that each of their 23 pupils in that group get half an hour each during that two-day time-slot. Once teachers have sat in on all presentations they can begin their half-term. There is no impact on the curriculum and teaching time because older pupils will be doing mocks at this time."

The student leads their conference, and the intention is that they do 85% of the talking/presenting, while the parents speaks for about 10% of the time, and the teacher 5%.

"The tutor's role is to intervene, prompt and remind if something is not being represented. The student-led conference is recorded on video, so the students can later reflect on their presentation skills. Done well, these conferences are extremely powerful."

(*continued*)

## Case study: Stanley Park High School, Carshalton (*continued*)

While a small number of parents continue to be reluctant to attend the conferences for their own reasons, the turn out generally has risen to well over 90%, compared with the 50% who came to the old-style parents' evenings.

> We used to ask parents what they thought about the conferences, but we are beyond that now as they are the established way we do things. We now ask them about their children's learning, for example, do they think their children are willing to take risks. In the future, we will expect pupils to talk more about outcomes, and aspects such as risk-taking, resilience, and what they find challenging.

Taylor sees the student-led conferences as a way of getting parents through the door.

> For many of them it will be the first time they've seen their children's books or sat down with them to discuss their work. This is about information-sharing, so it overcomes the awkwardness of a sullen child sitting there saying nothing.
>
> Here we have a detailed conversation, in school and under teacher supervision. It is a learning experience for the child and the parents.
>
> Often the student-led conferences are very moving because you might have a child with autism and limited communication telling their parents what they've been doing or exhibiting their work though art, acting or music. It is very powerful because the parents gain an understanding of what their children are learning, and this helps to engage them.

## Further reading

https://schoolleaders.thekeysupport.com/pupils-and-parents/engaging-parents-and-carers/pupil-reports-and-parents-evenings/parent-consultation-evenings-statutory-requirements/

www.teachertoolkit.co.uk/2016/02/21/parentsevenings/

DL

## Notes

1 http://dera.ioe.ac.uk/6639/1/DCSF-RW004.pdf
2 www.teachertoolkit.co.uk/2016/08/10/parental-support/
3 www.smf.co.uk/wp-content/uploads/2017/07/Education-Commission-final-web-report.pdf
4 http://dera.ioe.ac.uk/12136/1/download%3Fid%3D156367%26filename%3Dhow-to-involve-hard-to-reach-parents-full-report.pdf

# 6 Child protection and safeguarding

## Introduction

Child protection and safeguarding are potentially among the most difficult and sensitive subjects of discussion between schools and parents. They can often be the subject of disagreements and conflict between the two, sometimes to the detriment of the child.

Nevertheless, schools remain one of the front-line organisations for protecting children and young people, and child protection and safeguarding form a crucial aspect of their role.

When families refuse, or avoid, cooperating with schools on issues around safeguarding and child protection, it can result in serious problems for heads and teachers, who may need to seek outside help from social services, the police or other agencies. In some cases, it may be desirable that they do so rather than try to resolve complex issues on their own, and without appropriate training.

Schools, like other public bodies, have a wealth of guidance to refer to when dealing with child protection issues, but there will be times when they will need to weigh up the circumstances carefully before deciding the best course of action.

According to the UK government document *Working Together to Safeguard Children*,[1] safeguarding means protecting children from maltreatment, preventing impairment of children's health or development, ensuring that children grow up in circumstances consistent with the provision of safe and effective care and taking action to enable all children to have the best outcomes. Every aspect of this document applies to schools.

The definition is wide ranging and deliberately so. It encompasses the broad range of issues that have the potential to harm children's health, physical and emotional well-being and personal safety. In short, anything that impacts negatively on these aspects of a child's life is a child protection issue.

It can mean bullying, abuse in all its forms, neglect, involvement in gangs, exposure to extremism and radicalisation, trafficking, female genital mutilation or child marriage. Sometimes the actions of others can inadvertently put a child a risk. For example, being expelled from school, without appropriate follow-up support, can result in a child being vulnerable to mental health problems or getting involved in crime.

A failure by parents to engage with schools on child protection issues can take several forms. Parents may appear ambivalent by failing to attend meetings set up by the school or other agencies on safeguarding, or they avoid this contact by being constantly unavailable. In extreme cases, for example, they may appear compliant outwardly, but are planning to subvert the school's attempts to help the child, for example, in cases of forced marriage. However, some studies have shown that often they want to be involved but feel excluded and not listened to.

More recently, there have been growing concerns about the levels of mental health problems among young people, brought on by factors such as the pressures of school work and being academically successful, online bullying, addiction to gaming and social media and worries about the future, such as employment and housing.

## Exclusions

Exclusion from school is one of the biggest risks to school children's health and safety. Dr Martyn Walker, Principal Research Fellow at Huddersfield University's School of Education, believes that being removed from school has particular effects on young people's physical and emotional well-being.

He is aware of cases where children as young as five who are on the autistic spectrum have been excluded from schools because they were unable to cope with their specific needs.

> The rising rate of exclusions has only recently been brought into the public eye, and previously attempts would have been made to keep these children in the mainstream, A pupil referral unit would have been a last resort. Now children with special needs seem to be routinely excluded so they are out of sight of Ofsted inspectors and don't show up in examination results, which will affect league table rankings – a practice known as 'off-rolling'.
>
> It has become apparent that schools are not using exclusions in the context that they were supposed to be used for such as what would be defined as serious crimes such as violence against teachers and/or other pupils. Some schools are not taking advantage of employing additional teaching assistants, where children have a diagnosis, and instead seem to think that it is more convenient to exclude the pupil than to support them.
>
> Children who are permanently excluded and for whom no alternative provision is found often end up in gangs and are vulnerable to abuse and falling into crime. Often the parents just give up fighting the system or may not have the wherewithal to do so. Schools say it isn't their problem any longer and there is no advocacy for the young people.

He believes many of these problems could be avoided by schools having better relationships with parents, over and above their legal requirements to have a designated staff member responsible for leading on child protection.

"The idea of having a named and trained person – it doesn't have to be a teacher – who would have had the appropriate training, could support these 'at risk' children and their families and work with them in the role of a family liaison officer," he says.

> I know of one working in a special school who goes out to meet families in their homes to work with them and with the child in

the classroom, to provide strategies and solutions to the many challenges they face with issues such as substance abuse, domestic abuse, poverty and disadvantage.

Support plans are put in place to ensure that the children get the help they need, and to intervene before problems get out of hand. However, at the moment schools that offers this support have to submit bids to fund this service, for example, through lottery funding.

This should be extended to all schools and funded by government, as the long-term repercussions will prove to be substantially more expensive over a lifetime. It might include the state having to provide unemployment benefits, mental health support or funding the cost of imprisonment where a child has become disaffected with society.

Fears over the effects of exclusions on young people, and their parents, were explored by researchers at the University of Exeter who looked at exclusions from the perspective of parents. In a study published in 2016,[2] they examined the experiences of parents whose children had been excluded from school and found that how well the school communicated determined the child's ability to cope, and the way parents evaluated and made sense of what had happened.

Some felt their expertise and knowledge as parents of the child had not been taken into consideration, which then escalated the sense of blame between the parties. Others felt they were not listened to at all and their input was neither desired nor respected. This in turn made the parents feel apathetic and disengaged and sometimes led them to avoid communication with the school altogether, rather than be ignored.

Where communication was deemed to be good, parents were able to evaluate the school's decision and actions more positively and were in a better position to access help from other professionals, such as a helpful adviser, school counsellor or GP.

The study concluded that where communication between the school and home were good following a child's exclusion, the parents expressed more positive views of the school. "Ensuring timely and effective communication should be a priority for those working with children at risk of exclusion," the study says.

## Training and support

Organisations such as the NSPCC work closely with schools and other organisations around improving their safeguarding policies, practices and procedures. Among the organisation's biggest concerns is a rise in the number of calls to the Childline helpline about anxiety and self-harm. While physical bullying is decreasing, online abuse is going up. Personal friendships and relationships are also of huge concern to children and young people.

Kay Joel, senior consultant for education with the NSPCC's consultancy services, says schools must comply with statutory guidelines on keep children safe in schools and at a minimum all staff much know how to recognise, respond, report and refer concerns about child abuse and neglect. One of the challenges, she says, is being aware of the issues in the community and to react to them, and not to be distracted by generalisations. The risk of the radicalisation of young people in one part of the country, for example, will not apply to another. Similarly, not every housing estate has gangs and rural and coastal towns are as likely to experience drug problems as urban areas.

She says:

> Schools use the definitions of physical, sexual and emotional abuse and neglect that are contained in the document Working Together to Safeguard Children, and among these might be specific issues such as forced marriage, for example.
>
> As an organisation, we try to provide teachers with advice on what they must do and examples of good practice, which might mean signposting them to different organisations depending on the issue. Local problems aren't always about gangs and crime, so schools need to be careful not to be diverted into everything being about that.
>
> (Kay Joel, NSPCC, Telephone interview, August 20, 2018)

A solution might be to dedicate a staff member, possibly one who lives locally, working as a type of community liaison officer, talking to parents and others about what they've observed in their locality and finding out about any incidents that might affect the safety and well-being of pupils.

> We have a dedicated training team which runs general or bespoke courses in schools and at centres around their country. All Designated Safeguarding Leads in schools must be trained in their role every two years. This person must be a senior member of staff, and we have specific courses for people in this role.
>
> When it comes to advising schools on relationships with parents we always recommend [that] they are frank and honest about what the safeguarding policy is, and to have it readily available on the school website and as a hard copy. It is best practice to make it as transparent as possible, and so they are aware who the designated member of staff is with responsibility for this area of school life. Often schools are not explicit enough about these policies, or about the need to refer a child to other agencies, such as social services if there are concerns. Good practice is informing parents and working with them, unless to do so would put the child at greater risk.
>
> Schools are still seen as a hub for community cohesion, and a safe place for children. But while the role of schools in safeguarding children has grown in recent years, the resources to do this effectively has not kept up with the pace.

## Top tips for schools

- Ensure there is a designated senior staff member to lead on child protection and safeguarding.
- The school's individual policy on child protection should be prominently displayed on the school's website, in the main reception area and available as fliers to distribute as needed.
- Make sure all staff members know how to respond to, and report, any concerns over the safety and well-being of a pupil, and that there is a culture of seeking help and support.

- Be open and honest with parents about why, what, how and with whom information could be shared and seek their agreement, unless it is unsafe or inappropriate to do so (see case study on Co-op Academy of Leeds).
- Staff members have easy access to the designated person(s) and the senior leadership team if needed.
- Ensure that staff are updated on any changes to policy and practice.
- Ensure that staff understand that some information is shared on a need-to-know basis.
- School leaders understand that certain issues need to be kept confidential, and recognise that some staff members may live in the local community.
- Training and resources are provided to reinforce individual safeguarding roles and responsibilities.

## A parent's perspective

Caroline Stewart's son was 11 when he had what she now describes as 'the conversation' with her. She had suspected for some time that he was gay, but hearing her child acknowledge it made her proud of his self-awareness and confidence, especially as the revelation came at a time when many children were struggling with the onset of adolescence.

She had warned him about revealing his sexual orientation to a wider audience too soon, and for a couple of years Ben had kept his news to himself, even though many of his friends and classmates would not have been surprised.

The problems began when, in Year 9, he joined in a conversation about homophobia during a PSHE lesson and defended the rights of LGBT people to live as they wished, against a classmate who expressed 'disgust' at the idea.

"From that day on his life was made a misery by this boy," Stewart explains. "The bully was a known problem to teachers anyway, but he managed to coerce a group of boys, who had otherwise been friendly to Ben, to harass and intimidate him, suggesting he was danger to their safety and he might make a pass at them."

Living in a small town in Wales meant Ben was often referred to as the 'only gay in the village,' a reference to a camp Welsh character in the TV series, *Little Britain*.

The bullying began with name-calling and teasing, but soon moved on to shoulder barging him in corridors and going through his PE kit bag for signs of 'gay-ness.' It got worse the more Ben ignored it and refused to deny his true self. The crunch came when the boys photoshopped a photo of Ben in an apparent sexual act and posted it on social media.

"They were trying to get a reaction out of Ben with their bullying, but this went beyond anything like that. The photo was passed around the school and Ben was absolutely mortified. He told me he wanted to kill himself, though I didn't think he meant it. He was humiliated and embarrassed."

Stewart spoke to staff, who initially didn't grasp the seriousness of the situation, or the distress that Ben was feeling every time he went into school. She persisted with phone calls and face-to-face discussions with his form tutor. Eventually, she wrote a formal letter of complaint to the head and chair of governors after Ben stood shaking on the doorstep one morning refusing to go in, and the school finally mobilised. The bully and his gang were hauled before the head teacher with their parents and warned they faced exclusion.

"Some of the parents were angry and ashamed of their sons, and came to us to apologise, while other stood beside them claiming they had done nothing wrong. It seemed strange that views were so polarised in this day and age, but it revealed that many of these anti-gay prejudices probably originated at home."

At the request of the school, Stewart stepped in to help start a discussion among pupils in the upper school, contacting a local support group for LGBT teenagers to come in and talk to pupils about coming out, being gay and homophobia. Parents were also invited to attend the sessions and about a handful turned up – Stewart believes more out of curiosity about what would be discussed than to add to their knowledge. She says:

> The school wanted to show firstly that it was supporting Ben and that it wasn't going to tolerate this behaviour, but also that it was backing me as a parent. Watching your smart, bright, confident child crumple into a wreck because of bullying made me realise that it's a collective responsibility we all have to stamp it out.
>
> I didn't feel that I could leave this to the school to sort out on its own, as this was my son's life and self-worth that was under threat. I wanted some control over how we solved this problem, and the school was happy for me to be on board.
>
> Ben and I had discussed it and decided we wanted some sort of input into changing attitudes. He became directly involved in the workshop by standing up and telling everyone how he felt about being bullied, and how he came to realise he was gay. It was very powerful to watch. Many pupils got quite emotional and some of the bullies just sat with their heads down, looking at their feet as they listened.
>
> At the end of the session, one of the boys waited behind, gave Ben a fist pump and said "Sorry, man. What you just did took a lot of guts."
>
> Ben told him it must have taken guts to do what he just did, too.

## Case study 1: Co-op Academy of Leeds

When Harinder Kaur confided in pupils that she had had an arranged marriage, it opened up a whole new way of working with parents and families.

The young teacher, who joined the Co-op Academy of Leeds in 2009, suddenly found herself the go-to teacher for pupils who were experiencing their own cultural dilemmas, including forced

(*continued*)

**Case study 1: Co-op Academy of Leeds** (*continued*)

marriage, honour-based abuse, breast ironing and female genital mutilation.

Digging deeper into the lives of her students and the communities they came from, she also found youngsters vulnerable to grooming and other forms of abuse in what remains a disadvantaged and under-privileged part of inner-city Leeds.

Now, as the Academy's Social, Culture and Ethos Lead, she finds one of the most effective ways of getting messages through to parents is by channeling them through the pupils.

"We have 75 different languages spoken among the children in the school and immigrant children come here at all ages, often with little or no English," Kaur says.

> About half of our families are on benefits. So, while it is a challenging school, it is also a school where we want pupils to feel empowered and have some control over their lives, so they can make decisions for themselves.
>
> No-one here is telling them not to listen to their parents, or to betray the teaching of their religions but they need to know what British values and human rights are, and that there are other ways of living your life.

The Academy has a large safeguarding team of 12 staff members to deal with the many potential challenges affecting pupils. Issues around safeguarding are introduced in PHSE lessons, assemblies and tutor groups, where they are discussed openly and honestly. Charities and other organisations with specific areas of expertise are also invited into the school to lead workshops and discussions.

One workshop, for example, advised that young people being forcibly taken overseas to be married to put a spoon in their

(*continued*)

## Case study 1: Co-op Academy of Leeds (*continued*)

underwear so that it triggers a security alert and search, during which the child can confide in secret that they are at risk.

"Previously we were not open about these things, just like many schools aren't," Kaur says:

> Teachers are often scared of raising cultural and religious traditions for fear of offending communities or being deemed to be racist and not having the right dialogue. But we cannot hinder these young people in their life chances.
>
> Many issues, such as arranged and forced marriages, are so deeply embedded in the pupils' cultures that they don't question them. But we tell them that they are living in another country now and they can move forward with the times, and there are opportunities open to them.

The school does not request permission from parents to discuss subjects that might be contentious as there is an expectation that they will conform, but parents are free to attend assemblies and lessons to see what is being taught, and how. There is some reliance, and expectation, by Kaur that the children will discuss what they have been taught with their parents, who can raise it with her or senior colleagues if they have any concerns.

> A few parents have come in to object to what is being raised with their children but, so far, I have managed to discuss this with them, and to reassure them that their children need to be protected. I explain that they are now living in a country with different values. In the main, they understand that there is a basic level of knowledge and understanding their children need to go out into the world, safely and confidently.

(*continued*)

## Case study 1: Co-op Academy of Leeds (*continued*)

There are some cultural issues on which the school has been quite explicit with parents, however. Parents are made aware in newsletters, via the school website and through conversations, if needed, that female genital mutilation, if suspected, is a police matter and not just an incident logged by the school, and that forced marriages have been illegal in the UK since 2014.

The school works closely with organisations such as Karma Nirvana, which advises schools on appropriate methods and strategies when discussing issues like honour-based abuse or FGM with pupils and parents. The organisation has an emergency helpline for children who believe they are in danger.

Anup Manota, Operations Manager for Karma Nirvana, said children could be forced into marriage for something as innocuous – to most people – as wearing jeans, going to the cinema or being seen speaking in public with a boy or girl who is not one of their own family. Young people suspected of, or admitting to, being gay may also be forced into marrying so they do not dishonour or bring shame on their families.

He says schools are often ill-prepared, and teachers inadequately trained, to deal with the complexities of these issues and the realisation that it is close family members who may be perpetuating them, because this truth is so alien to the British culture. Delivering assemblies in secondary schools, he says, often results in a flood of referrals.

> In one school a girl had her phone confiscated when she was caught using it during a lesson and she was told by teachers that her parents would be informed.
>
> The school ignored her pleas not to tell her parents, because they weren't aware she had a mobile phone, and went ahead and informed the family anyway. A few days later,

(*continued*)

## Case study 1: Co-op Academy of Leeds (*continued*)

> we were contacted by a desperate headteacher because the girl had gone missing and did not turn up to school after the incident.
>
> We went through our caller records to see if she had contacted us, but she hadn't, so we advised that the police be informed. We aren't sure to this day what happened to her.

The incident illustrates that there are occasions when teachers need to be discreet about what information they pass on to parents and family members because they may inadvertently be putting a child in greater danger.

"Often parents act normally in these situations when confronted by the school and don't give anything away about what they are planning. But then the child suddenly moves school, or is taken abroad without anyone being told," Manota adds.

> There is statutory guidance on forced marriage that the school can share with parents, which is backed up by legislation, which might make some families think twice about their actions.
>
> We would always advise schools to train their teachers or ask our advice before trying to tackle these situations. There is support out there, and teachers like Harinder have managed to balance the trust side with being able to help children.

Kaur believes that her own background, as a young Sikh woman who has had an arranged marriage, has encouraged the trust and confidence among parents that their children will not be drawn into areas and subjects of discussion that are inappropriate, or go against their religious and cultural traditions.

(*continued*)

## Case study 1: Co-op Academy of Leeds (*continued*)

"There should be a teacher in every school who leads on cultural and religious issues and builds up the trust and understanding of parents, and pupils," Kaur says. "Currently there is no requirement on schools to tackle these matters, but there should be as we know there are safe-guarding problems affecting many pupils in our schools. I would go as far as to say that it is something that Ofsted should be looking at."

The key, she says, is to keep returning to the issues rather than treating them as subjects that are re-visited and discussed occasionally when the need arises. This sends out a message to parents, and pupils, that these topics form part of the ethos of the school and are not just an add-on when something goes wrong or a specific situation prompts the school into action. She continues:

> By talking about this regularly, it means the children take this information home and talk about it with their parents. This has become our main channel of communication because, although we have interpreters in school, it is the children who bring this up at home and the parents will see we are not against their religion by what their children say.
>
> Hopefully it is opening the minds of the parents, just as our approach is doing so with the pupils.

**Advice on dealing with honour-based abuse and other cultural behaviours**

- Believe what the child is telling you and listen to them.
- Be aware of historical behaviour within the family, such as the forced marriage of a sibling, as this increases the chance of it being repeated.

(*continued*)

## Case study 1: Co-op Academy of Leeds (*continued*)

- Restrict the information you share about incidents in school as you may be putting a child in further danger.
- Be careful about using interpreters. Sometimes the victim, or a close family member, is used to interpret and may not give honest responses.
- Do not try to mediate on behalf of the child, as you need specific training in this. Usually it is the family carrying out the abuse and there might be a wider network involved as well.
- Use the helpline of Karma Nirvana or contact the local authority or police if you have concerns.

## Case study 2: John Perryn Primary School, Acton, London

When Branwen Hywel joined John Perryn Primary School in 2011, friends and colleagues asked her why she wanted to take on such a challenging school. Seven years on, and it is among the top 1% of schools in terms of progress in terms of attainment.

The road to get here was long and sometimes rocky, as she explains. "There was a complete lack of trust in the school at the time I joined, and I think much of it was justified. We had an enormous task on our hands to build up the school's reputation and to show children here that they are capable and could achieve."

One of the challenges was to make the school, based in Ealing, west London, a safer place. A highly ethnically diverse school, about 65% of pupils at John Perryn are Muslim, many of them

(*continued*)

## Case study 2: John Perryn Primary School, Acton, London (*continued*)

refugees, and 10% Travellers, and Roman Catholics. The rest of the children come from mainly immigrant backgrounds, with only three children in each year group of 60 coming from white British homes.

"Some of the groups didn't like each other and it wasn't uncommon to hear the racist and homophobic language they use in their own communities coming into school," she explains.

> I was flabbergasted at some of the things I was hearing and the term 'gay' seemed to be used by everyone, including staff and children, as an accepted term of abuse.
>
> At that time, the police would be called regularly when fighting broke out and it was quite simply a case of different cultures clashing. Traveller families seem to be the one ethnic group that people feel it's still ok to abuse, and there were different levels of acceptance among families of what were and were not acceptable words to use to refer to each other.
>
> Some communities demanded tolerance but didn't show it themselves for others. So, at the end of the day we'd have Somali families standing together and turning their backs on everyone and being distrustful, Travellers parked on double yellow lines and not caring whether they got a parking ticket, and the white British just generally disliking everyone.
>
> (Bronwen Hywel, John Perryn Primary School, May 24, 2018)

Hywel set about raising trust and respect among the different groups by modelling exceptional behaviour at all times. The introduction of a school ethos, known as The John Perryn Way,

(*continued*)

## Case study 2: John Perryn Primary School, Acton, London (*continued*)

offered the whole-school community a template for good behaviour that is still used today, with the motto *Aim High to Gain Success in Everything We Do.*

> Even now, if I walk down the school drive I might hear children saying "quick, do the John Perryn Way!" when they see me. It's about treating everyone with respect and tolerance, respecting their right to be here as part of our school and learning and taking responsibility for one's own actions. It has made our school a fun and caring place to be which is what we live and die for here.

Hywel then began the process of trying to bring communities closer together.

> We had to do this step by step. A Parent-Teacher-Families Association was set up to get parents and carers into school to show them how their children learn and what teachers' expectations are, and to get them involved in the life of the school generally.
>
> We would have cake sales and invite them in for tea and coffee. Only three Somali mums came to the first one, but now they are well-attended.
>
> We realised that we needed to show that every community group was equally valued, so we mark every religious holiday. During Eid, some of the Somali community made food for everyone to try and people came along because they were interested in trying it. So that broke the ice. We also started to organise a Christmas fayre and observe other festive days during the year so that everyone felt a part of the

(*continued*)

## Case study 2: John Perryn Primary School, Acton, London (*continued*)

> school community and valued equally. We expect everyone to show respect and understanding to others.

Some of the Traveller families were harder to convince to come into school. So, instead, coffee mornings took place on their site, and Hywel remains one of a handful of non-Travellers allowed on their property. She is also unique in being one of very few head teachers in the country who fines Travellers for non-attendance at school, except for authorised absences to two of their own annual events.

> Everyone here needs to show why they aren't in school, and this doesn't necessarily make me popular. We have more Travellers than most schools, so frequent unauthorised absences would show in our school attendance figures. We have an expectation that everyone has a right to learn and to achieve, and you can only do that by being in school.

John Perryn also began to offer learning classes for the parents, gently coaxing them into school when reluctant. "Parents often feel they don't have much to offer children if they've had a bad experience of school themselves. Some of the communities also have low levels of literacy, and parents don't want to admit this."

Courses were offered to help parents understand how their children were being taught, particularly in maths, with interpreters being brought in to help Arabic, Somali and Polish speakers. If Travellers declined to come to school, then the sessions were delivered on their site.

Other workshops offered by John Perryn were focused on safeguarding. Parents were sign-posted to services at their local

(*continued*)

## Case study 2: John Perryn Primary School, Acton, London (*continued*)

children's centre, and school-based 'stay and play' sessions helped families to settle into the school and to develop their understanding of what was expected, both academically and socially. Parents were able to access counselling services through the same provision as the art and play therapy delivered to pupils who needed it. Workshops were also provided in internet safety and relationships and sex education, and generally in how to keep children safe.

> In a majority of Muslim and Traveller families, homosexuality is frowned upon, at best, so while we are careful not to insult their beliefs we also have to make clear that these are legal and acceptable relationships in this country between loving people, and that in this society these relationships are acceptable.
>
> These sessions may also include discussion about female genital mutilation, as we are based in a high-risk borough in terms of the communities who live here and locally there have been cases of children as young as six disappearing. Where we have suspicions we refer them to the local Prevent Team, which we have had to do a few times when children reveal they are unexpectedly going on holiday.
>
> There have been occasions where I have had to speak to families and ask where they are going and what they are doing, and then spoken to social services if I remain concerned.
>
> Sometimes parents will ask for their children to be opted out of sex and relationships education. Usually these requests come from Muslim or Traveller families, in which children tend to marry early and sex isn't discussed, and there is a gender input into relationships. Considering these were groups that traditionally didn't like each other, they do have a lot in common.

(*continued*)

## Case study 2: John Perryn Primary School, Acton, London (*continued*)

Having set about uplifting a school where there was distrust and disharmony, Hywel now presides over an orderly and purposeful community of pupils, teachers and families, all working together.

> We now get great results and as well as making excellent progress, our pupils leave here with good learning habits and confidence. We have done this by creating a safe, secure environment for children to learn and be together.
>
> All of this combined will help them achieve what they want to in life.

## Further reading

https://assets.publishing.service.gov.uk/government/uploads/system/uploads/attachment_data/file/721581/Information_sharing_advice_practitioners_safeguarding_services.pdf
https://karmanirvana.org.uk/
https://learning.nspcc.org.uk/safeguarding-child-protection-schools/
www.gov.uk/government/publications/keeping-children-safe-in-education-2
www.gov.uk/government/publications/what-to-do-if-youre-worried-a-child-is-being-abused-2
www.rip.org.uk/news-and-views/latest-news/working-with-parents-to-safeguard-children-from-cse/

DL

## Notes

1 https://assets.publishing.service.gov.uk/government/uploads/system/uploads/attachment_data/file/729914/Working_Together_to_Safeguard_Children-2018.pdf
2 www.tandfonline.com/doi/full/10.1080/13632752.2015.1120070

# 7 Special needs and disabilities

## Introduction

There can surely be no greater need for teachers and parents to collaborate and work closely together than with children who have special educational needs and disabilities (SEND).

Jointly agreed strategies and approaches to learning, behaviour and emotional support are vital if a child is to succeed and thrive. But because of the complexities and sensitive nature of SEND, these relationships can often be strained with the school and family having conflicting ideas of what is best for the child and how this can be achieved.

According to UK government statistics[1] the number and proportion of pupils classified as having SEND has been gradually declining since 2010, due in most part to changes in statementing. Around 14.4% or 1.23 million pupils in England are SEND, and of these some 237,000 have a statement or an education health and care plan (EHCP). In Wales[2] there were 105,577 pupils with special educational needs in maintained schools, or 22.6% of all pupils, while in Scotland, where it is referred to as requiring additional special support, the proportion is 26.6%,[3] and in Northern Ireland[4] it is 23%.

So, there are millions of children and families living with the problems, worries and trauma of SEND in a high-stakes and highly accountable education system led by governments focused on outcomes and statistics.

Pupils' needs can be many and varied, with extreme levels of severity. A child presenting with one learning difficulty may often display others too, requiring specific expertise and input from teaching staff. Their parents, too, may have special needs or have suffered the grief of having a child with special needs.

Lorraine Petersen, a former head teacher and now a leading educational consultant specialising in SEND, who has worked with schools and the teachers of special needs for 40 years, believes that while relationships between teachers and parents are vital to the child's future success, they can be fraught with difficulties because of the complexities and sensitivities involved. An increase in mental health problems among young people all over the country is adding to these challenges:

> As a profession we know far more about special needs and disabilities than we ever have before, but we also have children and young people growing up with pressures that previous generations didn't have, which are adding to mental health needs.
>
> Essentially, what we have is a 20th century profession, trained in 20th century pedagogy and a 20th century curriculum trying to cater for 21st century children. These are complex problems.
>
> (Lorraine Petersen, February 1, 2018)

"One of the issues is that the special educational needs coordinators (Senco) and teachers are often not adequately trained on how to work with parents," Petersen says:

> while parents are themselves often aware and savvy because they have spent months or years battling with the system to get the children they help and support they need.
>
> Not only are teachers not trained on how to work with and collaborate with parents, but they may not fully understand or have knowledge of the many complex needs a child may have as they go through the school system. It's not uncommon for teachers will give a label to a particular behaviour without knowing how to identify what the underlying causes are.

The new education, health and care plans (EHCP) now in place in parts of the UK, which were introduced by The Children and Families

Act 2014,[5] are more focused on outcomes for children and young people than in the provision itself. Whatever plan is drafted for a learner will include a list of their learning difficulties and impairments, and what this means for them personally. A good plan will include a list of provisions to meet the child's needs, and every provision should result in an outcome for the child.

Some of these provisions will be what schools call 'ordinarily available' and are offered by the school anyway. Resources and provision over and above this will be funded by the local authority to provide additional support. For example, a child who requires regular speech and language therapy should be funded by the local authority as part of the child's plan.

In addition, parents can seek a personal budget which is for anything that is deemed necessary and not available from the school, but might support an outcome within the plan. For example, a parent may believe that riding therapy is good for their child who has autism and, while the school will not offer this, the parent can seek a personal budget from the local authority to pay for it.

Peterson says:

> Some local authorities will have their own policies which may not follow SEND law. In this case they tell schools that if they're giving money to the parents through a personal budget then that must come out of what additional funding the school receives. This is not the case, however – personal budgets are the responsibility of the local authority. It takes savvy parents to battle through the system, go to tribunals and fight for what their child needs.
>
> Under the new arrangements, parents have a great deal of power and must be involved in the writing of their EHCP for their children. They know their child and his or her needs best. Schools, local authorities and other professionals should co-produce the EHCP with the parents and child at the heart of the discussions. The parents are the lead and have a lot of rights. Often the school does the drafting of the paperwork necessary for an EHCP needs assessment, but it can be initiated by the parents.
>
> So, it is in the interests of the school always to work closely with the parents, though some remain reluctant to do this.

For parents, discovering that their child has a learning disability can come as a shock. Raising this possibility with a parent early on can reduce the trauma and give the parents knowledge and some control over what happens next. Teachers should be talking about the child's potential challenges and problems before a label or diagnosis is introduced.

Petersen says the following:

> The whole point of the SEND Code of Practice is that parents must be informed at the point the school decides there is a SEND. A school will have done a lot of work with a child before arriving at the conclusion there is a special need and the parent should have been involved in this from day one.
>
> Schools also need to be asking questions of early years settings, and secondary schools of primary schools.

But there are also questions that need to be asked that only the parent, with their experience of giving birth to and raising the child in their first months and years, can answer. Was this child premature? Was the child conceived by IVF? Was there any early trauma in their life? Were there bonding and attachment issues at birth because the child was in an incubator?

"All of these issues can have a huge impact on a child's early development, and would be useful for a school to know," Petersen says.

> Parents could be given a written questionnaire to answer in reception answering questions such as these because all these issues matter and could have a bearing on the child's development.
>
> For example, a child who was due in November but born in August is not only premature but summer-born and may have a disability such as a hearing impairment as a result of being born early. Children who are premature may be pre-disposed to having a special need or disability.
>
> We now have babies being born at 26 weeks and surviving, and they are developing outside the uterus, which also has an impact on their development.

Another question with implications is around multiple births. There have been cases of twins being born following conception through IVF where one was later found to have significant special needs, possibly caused by their positioning in the womb.

"The more we know about modern medical science the more children are surviving, but with this comes consequences around children's health and implications on their development," Petersen says.

> For many parents, a child being born with a disability is a bereavement as they have not got the baby they hoped for, but this precious child is here and is loved by the parents, and the school must understand this. Parents might be going through a real trauma with this child.
>
> We are not training teachers to deal with these situations, and the barriers go up in schools because no one knows how to deal with it or what to do. Teachers often say they see angry parents, but these are families who need support.
>
> Resolving some of these issues would make relationships easier for everyone in school – the child, the teachers and the other pupils and the parent would be happier too. Everyone is going through this and trying to do what's best for the child – so why would you not want to work together?

In special schools the communication between parents and school tends to be very strong and most of it is done externally because the children are taken in by bus or taxi. A home-school diary or the use of e-mail helps teachers and parents to stay in contact. In mainstream primary, it is easy to stay in contact because parents come to the school twice a day to drop off and pickup their children. But that contact tails off once children start secondary school.

In order to maintain close links, schools should consider having a parent liaison worker specifically for this purpose. "Research has shown that children who come from a home where there is anxiety come into school anxious," Petersen says. "New ways of teaching can be confusing for parents as they were taught differently. A parent liaison worker could smooth some of those anxieties, ensure the child is being provided for, and that the parents understand about the curriculum and what their child is being taught."

Another issue increasingly affecting pupils with special needs is qualification reform. The new focus on more difficult, traditional subjects means that, in many schools, there are fewer opportunity to take subjects such as art, music, drama and design and technology. "Schools need to ensure they are providing for these children as 'parent power' means they can vote with their feet and go elsewhere," Petersen says.

"Some schools are now saying to Year 5 and 6 pupils moving to secondary that they can't meet that child's needs, so they need to look elsewhere, even though they have no way of knowing this until they've tried. What they are saying is 'your child will bring down our results'. Parents will then think twice about sending them to that school, but they need to know that a school cannot turn down a child because their needs can't be met. It is part of the admissions code, but parents get bamboozled by what schools are telling them."

From a school's perspective, the parents of children with special needs usually fall into a number of categories:

- **The parents who are constantly in school, wanting to help and pressuring the teacher to do more.**

These parents often press for further assessments and are keen to get an EHCP for their child, even if the child doesn't meet the local authority criteria for a needs assessment. Sometimes they don't fully understand the SEND system and how it works, and school needs to be clear about roles, responsibilities and duties.

Local authorities have tended to set up their own internal policies relating to the assessment for SEND that do not necessarily strictly follow the law. Schools will often follow the local authorities' guidelines because they don't understand the law themselves. So, schools – and parents – need to be clear about the law, and not just what the local authority guidelines say as these are an interpretation of the law.

Where relationships work best, schools, local authorities and parents are all clear on what their roles and responsibilities are and are working together to best support the child. Parents need to understand that there are criteria for eligibility for a plan which their child may not meet. The school needs to communicate effectively that this is the case, and this is the role of the Senco, which every school must have by law.

Where a school has noticed that a child has fallen behind and has undertaken internal assessments with a view to identifying a special need, parents must be informed. The child is then added to the SEND register and will receive additional support for their identified need. The school must offer three progress meetings a year with pupils and parents. The parents should be made aware of this, and they have a right to ask why they aren't getting progress meetings about their child. Sustaining this relationship may be more challenging in secondary school, especially if the Senco doesn't know the child well.

- **The parent seeking to get a diagnosis or label for their child, so they can access additional benefits, or health or social care support. The school may not believe the support is needed but the parent pushes for this for their own reasons.**

There are a number of reasons why a parent may want a 'label' for their children. It could be to get additional benefits or other support, or to secure access arrangements in examinations. This usually means additional time being agreed by the awarding bodies to complete the papers, or some sort of assistance given in examinations.

However, this must have been the child's normal way of working for at least two years previously, to deter parents from trying to secure these arrangements just prior to tests and examinations.

How does the school deal with this? Petersen says the following:

> It tends to be the better off parents who get education psychology reports done, often at a cost of hundreds of pounds, and it is fair to say that when parents are paying the psychologist might side with them. These reports are then presented to the school, which might say that this is not the child they know and recognise. It is in the school's interests to work with the parent before it gets to that stage.

- **Parents who are in denial, who do not accept their child might be having difficulties and refuse to be put on EHCP or to receive specialist support. In most extreme cases this may be considered neglect and a child protection issue.**

Teachers may be telling the parents that they have noticed their child isn't behaving as they would expect or have noticed that things are not well with their level of progress, but the parents haven't noticed because the child is not displaying any outward signs at home of anything being amiss.

The way to communicate to parents who may be in denial is not to use the words 'special needs' in the first instance but to use language that doesn't label them. Showing sensitivity in this situation will make it easier to get the parents on side and to cooperate with any diagnostic assessment that need to be carried out.

Petersen says:

> This is potentially a very difficult situation because the reaction, or lack of it, from the parents could be deemed neglect of the child.
>
> For example, if as a school if you want to get special support from an educational psychologist then the parents have to give permission for this. If they refuse and the child's behaviour deteriorates, it could become a safe-guarding issue, and from the school's perspective might be perceived as neglect.
>
> Parents need to understand that if the school spots a problem then they need to work with the teachers and the school. This is why teachers need to be trained to work and how to talk to parents.

Schools may not act without the say-so of the parents, and this is the key. In most areas of the country, local authorities have cut services and no longer provide support services such as education welfare officers who would fulfil certain roles. It means that schools must now have a system in place for finding the best way to engage with families, whether this is visiting the child's home, or meeting with parents on neutral ground.

"Schools are also having to manage absences when parents decide they're going to take the child out of the school and home educate," Petersen says. "More children than ever with SEND are being home educated or are just not in education because their parents are refusing to send them to the setting named in their plan. The biggest group of the most vulnerable children are often those who are not in school."

Where parents persistently refuse to engage with the school on the well-being of their child, the school may have to report this to social services as a safeguarding issue, especially if they believe the child is at risk. In such cases the parents have to be informed, even if consent is not needed.

With people now using technology to communicate, it could be that schools have to get better at using technology to keep parents informed through the use of e-mail, text messaging or via apps that provide information and links about the activities in school.

"The good old-fashioned ways like inviting them in for a chat, and a coffee and a biscuit,are also effective and give parents the time and opportunity to talk," Petersen says. "As the relationship progresses and parents becoming more accepting of their child's needs, it might be worth offering workshops in areas like anger management or mindfulness, which will also help to get them into school."

- **Parents who are not honest about problems or behaviour taking place at home that would help the school to know so that they can support the child.**

Sometimes parents aren't honest about what the child is like at home because they believe it might reflect on their parenting skills. There may be problems at home that can affect a child, such as bereavement, marriage break-up, a sick relative or a sibling with substance abuse, for example. There might also be mental health issues in the family.

Schools might consider training up a teaching assistant or assigning a teacher who has experience in mentoring or counselling who could extract this information sensitively, and without making the parent feel they are to blame. This would build trust and confidence in the school and start the conversation about what difficulties the child is facing and how the school and parents can work together.

All local authorities must offer an independent support group whose members are able to guide parents through the EHCP process, will go to tribunals with them and seek redress and offer advice and guidance so families do not feel alone.

## Gifted and talented pupils

Many educationalists consider children who have particular gifts, talents and exceptional ability in English and/or mathematics to have special needs, since schools may have to differentiate and use different means of meeting their needs in the classroom.

Children falling into this category used to be referred to officially as 'gifted and talented' and, under previous governments, schools were expected to keep a register of pupils who displayed particularly aptitude and abilities. Some schools considered the top 10% of achievers in numeracy and literacy to fall into this category, while others also listed students with exceptional abilities in sport, music or other disciplines.

Schools now use the label less, but gifted children may display traits other than their academic abilities of which teachers and parents should be aware.

They may, for example, find it difficult to relate to others and make friends, especially if they are aware from the comments of parents or teachers that they are 'different.' They may also find it hard to concentrate, or display a lack of motivation in class if they aren't adequately stretched or challenged and find the work too easy.

If they are used to excelling in class, they may suffer from anxiety or fear of failure if they cannot sustain the expectations of them by their parents or teachers.

It should be remembered, too, that gifted and talented children may also have special needs, such as ADHD or be on the autistic spectrum.

Dr Ruth Hewston, Head of Department for Education and Inclusion at the University of Worcester, has studied the concept of gifted and talented – or learners of high ability as she prefers to describe them – and believes that they require similar levels of attention to any other child with special needs.

"Many of the studies around the engagement with school of parents who have able children is in their role in nomination," she says. "By that we mean they are the ones who identify in the first instance a particular gift or ability their child has and may point this out to the school."

Many talents displayed by young people are evident to the parents, but not to the school because they manifest in out of school clubs or other activities. Schools, on the other hand, having identified a child as gifted might decide not to share that information with parents for a number of reasons.

"A child might appear to excel at maths in primary school, but be found to be unexceptional in secondary, because their ability is relative to the cohort," Hewston says.

> Faith schools are often hesitant in labelling children because they prefer to believe that every child has a gift or ability.
>
> What is also problematic is that schools tend to use ability in literacy and numeracy as a benchmark, and wouldn't really label a child as exceptional in history or geography, in the same way.
>
> (Ruth Hewston, Telephone interview, September 7, 2018)

Hewston believes that dialogue is needed between schools and parents to best serve the needs of pupils of exceptional ability, and both need to listen to the other.

"A parent with a child who, for example, has a reading age above and beyond their chronological age might want more difficult reading materials for their child, but they need to remember this might not always be suitable for their age," she says.

Differentiation may also prove counterproductive with a child who doesn't want to be labelled as academically successful, for social or other reasons.

"There is a risk of able pupils being turned off learning if they are given additional or different work and playing down their abilities, so they are not singled out and made to feel different, or because they simply don't want extra school work to do."

## Parents fighting the system

Four years ago, Emilie-Kate Kidd and core group of other families set up Parents in Need[6] after they each spent thousands of pounds seeking a diagnosis of special educational needs for their children – a process that involved the hiring of lawyers and barristers.

In Kidd's case, she has spent several tens of thousands of pounds securing the appropriate education for her son, who has a severe speech and language disorder, muscular problems and global developmental delay.

She relates the following:

> My son was placed in an inappropriate school for him, for children with learning, social and communication problems. He is desperate to communicate with those around him, so we took him out of the school after four days because he was inconsolable and spent 6 months with him at home while we fought the LA for an appropriate school.
>
> That is the problem here – local authorities tend not to assess comprehensively enough, and the assessment system is too superficial. They then allocate children a place in a school that might not be suitable, and the schools are instructed to cope in whatever way they can. All too often these children are offered no specialist provision at all and are expected to go to a mainstream school.
>
> It can cost up to £6,000 for parents to get the necessary assessments carried out on their child, such as educational psychology, occupational therapy and speech and language therapy, and taking the LA to tribunal can be a costly process, as we found. The LA refused to reply to us, only to our lawyer so, unfortunately, legal representation was a costly necessity.

(*continued*)

## Parents fighting the system (*continued*)

> For us, comprehensive assessment meant everything, and we were shocked when the private Educational Psychologist told us that once she had removed the tests impeded by his speech and language disorder and motor skills, she discovered that he had an age appropriate cognitive ability. This explained why the initial school placement was such a disaster. He is now at a speech and language school and learning sign language. Without the assessments he would still be at a school for learning disabilities and autism and would still have no method, or peers with whom to communicate.
>
> (Emilie-Kate Kidd, Telephone interview, September 10, 2018)

Parents in Need now helps families with the assessment costs, so that more children and young people with special educational needs and disabilities can gain access to the appropriate provision. Its referrals come from another charity called SOS! SEN, which runs a helpline for parents struggling to navigate the complex SEND system.

Parents in Need employs the services of educational psychologists, OTs and SALTs who have a good reputation in their field and whose reports are recognised by tribunal panels as being robust and accurate, so that the funds are well spent.

Kidd stresses that it is the processes used by local authorities, and not schools, that are to blame for many SEND children being sent to the wrong setting. But she adds:

> There are many things that teachers can do to help with the process.
>
> Teaching staff should document and record any evidence they see of something not being quite right about a child,

(*continued*)

**Parents fighting the system** (*continued*)

and any suspicions they may have that a child may have a particular need.

Then they should talk to the school special education needs and disabilities coordinator (Sendco) and consider making a referral to a specialist service, for example speech and language, or occupational therapy. Teachers often don't realise they have the power to do this.

Try to be empathetic to a parents' concerns and listen to them. No parent wants there to be something wrong with their child, and they may be going through the bereavement of accepting their child has a special need and are fearful for their future. Having a child with special needs places enormous strains on a marriage and about 80% of marriages in this situation experience divorce.

It's also possible that the child's needs are not being met at home, and other agencies, such as social care, may need to be involved. Most boroughs have a Children With Disabilities Team who only oversee a fraction of the children with SEND in their borough, but the school can make a referral to this team.

## A parent's perspective – Barbara Kenny

Barbara Kenny's son, Robert has 'lots going on.' The eldest of three children, the 11 year-old has multiple learning difficulties, including autism, ADHD and dyslexia.

Robert is currently in a unit attached to a mainstream school, but this is his eighth setting since he began in the education system at the age of three years. He had an early diagnosis of autism at the age of two years and three months.

"When he went to nursery at the age of three, we realised no one knew how to deal with his needs," Barbara explains. "Not only was the experience and expertise lacking among the staff, but no-one was listening to us and that was really difficult."

Barbara did a National Autistic Society course, which she paid for herself, to learn more about speech and language, and occupational, therapy to find out how she could help her son. By the time Robert went to pre-school and nursery, she had had 15 hours of training.

> It was a course specifically for the parents of children with autism. For example, I learned that he had to do things for himself. So, if I gave him a yogurt I didn't take off the lid – he had to do this himself.
>
> Because I got information like this really early, I was able to work with him from a young age. But when you take your child to a setting you realise no one has had this sort of training.
>
> The whole child-led agenda is very difficult for children with autism. Robert was unable to decide for himself or to choose what he was doing and this was very frustrating.

Despite his learning difficulties, Robert was expected to meet the targets of the early years foundation stage (EYFS) like every other child. Barbara noticed that, in one setting, Robert rang a bell continuously for 20 minutes and that this was 'ticked off' in his EYFS record to show that he had engaged with a musical instrument. Meanwhile, running a car up and down a radiator was accepted as demonstrating imaginative play.

At another setting, Robert had a teaching assistant and one-to-one attention for most of the time, but Barbara felt that he made little progress. "Their primary concern seemed to be to keep him happy and content, and I didn't really see him making any progress academically. So, he was getting little benefit from being in what was supposed to be a learning environment."

Barbara was also offered tutors to teach Robert at home, who were keen to offer Barbara respite from her son:

> The problem was that I knew how to help Robert better than they did, because of my training. What I really needed was for someone

> to take my baby daughter away for a few hours, so I could devote my time to Robert. It wasn't him I needed respite from. I wanted to work with him.
>
> Parents are often seen as victims who need time away from their disabled child.

Barbara also did the Hanen speech and language course aimed at parents[7] which enhanced her knowledge of what Robert's needs were, but this only reinforced how much less the teachers in his school knew.

"It was becoming more and more frustrating," she says. "The teachers had very little training and I was telling them what was needed but I expected professionals to know this. They didn't really listen to what I was suggesting, and they wouldn't attempt to do anything they hadn't had training in."

What Barbara wanted was for Robert to 'do' things. She suggested to the staff in one nursery that they allow him to give out fruit to his classmates at break-times. This would have required him to ask which piece of fruit they wanted, listen to the reply and respond accordingly. The repetition of doing this with 30 children would have encouraged him to learn. But the staff said he could only do this with one child every day. "It felt like a missed opportunity and he learned much slower than he would have done otherwise," Barbara adds.

Robert's learning difficulties also had an impact on his behaviour, and as he become older it was apparent that he was often distracted by earrings and pony tails in girls' hair. This meant that a good place for him to be seated would have been at the front of the class where he couldn't see other children. "But instead he was placed at the back because that's where the TA sat with the disruptive children," Barbara says.

She believes that teachers often believe that, as professionals, they know best and are supposed to know best, and it can be difficult to convince them that other approaches may be effective.

> It seems to me that a lot of teachers never get around to putting in interventions for the special needs or disabled children because there are so many distractions and demands on their time, and that child is never the priority.

> There are also low expectations of children like Robert. In one setting, they didn't think he could put his shoes on, but he could already do this. Staff said that some skills would not necessarily be transferred from the home to school, which seemed daft to me.
>
> And once you start complaining you get a reputation for being a moaning parent who is constantly unhappy with what the school is doing. I often felt that teachers didn't ask enough about Robert and what he was capable of, and what he was doing at home. There was so much information I could have shared – I could have told them for example, that while he was clever he is also very lazy.

Barbara says the pattern of not listening to her suggestions of Robert's needs was repeated in most settings he went to. "There was often too much time spent on life skills, and not enough on reading and writing," she says. She began teaching him more and more herself at home but continued to send him to school so he could be with other children.

Eventually, and after home-educating Robert for a year at home, the family moved to another authority and Barbara found a school she could work with and which suited her son's needs. The school had an autism unit and used Robert's motivations and interests to get him back on track.

> During our visit the head was very honest and transparent about the school, and that it didn't necessarily have the expertise, but he welcomed Robert in. The main thing was the staff working with Robert listened to me. I gave them the data I had collected during the year I home-schooled, and they didn't just toss it to one side but used it to set levels and targets.
>
> They made extra time for speech and language therapy, and involved me in every step, while always explaining the constraints they were under.
>
> Between us, we worked out what was needed and what the best course of action would be. We worked on the positive strategies we could use. This included sending home work that I could do with him, so there was continuity.

The outcome of this has been phenomenal. He has made up 1.5–2 years progress.

Barbara says that parents of children with special needs are constantly told by teachers that they know their child best but often don't draw on that knowledge.

"We spend our lives problem-solving and trying to motivate our children, tapping into what works and what doesn't. This is valuable information. Teachers should use it."

## Top tips for engaging with parents

- Give parents lots of information about the child's day at school. Unlike children who develop normally, SEND children aren't always able to have a conversation with their parents to share their experience of the day, which disadvantages parents in terms of advocacy. Don't be reluctant to share this information.
- When taking the child out of their usual environment, such as a school trip, report back on what happened and how the child responded to a different setting. It's important for parents to know how it went and how their child coped.
- Trust parents to make a value judgement for which is right for their child. Robert's parents were told he'd never be able to write, he actually has amazing hand-writing.
- Be accountable to parents. They just want to help in the learning process and to be involved.
- Listen to what parents have to say and the strategies they know work. You need to find joint solution to problems.
- Do what you can to meet the child's needs in terms of the resources they need.
- Start the transition process from one school, or one sector, to another early so that staff can plan ahead and meet the pupil's needs on arrival. This might include planning logistics around the school to accommodate a wheelchair or providing appropriate staff training.

## Priestnall School case study

There are no decisions or strategies implemented for special needs children attending Priestnall School that do not directly involve consultation or the agreement of parents or carers.

And these discussions begin early. Gareth Morewood, the school's Special Needs Coordinator, instigates a dialogue with families whose children are in Years 4 and 5 in primary school to establish early on an understanding of the family, its circumstances and the individual challenges facing the child.

By the time the children arrive at Priestnall, which is based in Stockport, the school will know all about the children and be ready to meet their needs with agreed plans and provision.

"We are very focused on the individual and ensure support and special education provision is tailored to the specific plans for the child," Morewood explains. "We believe this is the only way to do it – though personalisation, and not normalisation. I often hear schools saying, 'this is what we do for children with autism' but all they have seen is one child and not understood that every child is unique, and plans must be personal to them as an individual.

"We understand why there might be a multiple of reasons why parents are not engaged with school."

> They might have had a difficult time at school themselves or simply poor responses from previous settings. It is not unusual for some parents to have additional needs themselves which weren't identified or addressed during their education and are only now coming to terms with their own needs having never done so in school.
>
> We also have children who are looked-after or adopted, and parents raising their children on their own. Regardless of

(*continued*)

## Priestnall School case study (*continued*)

> the circumstances, these are all families and parents or carers trying to do the best for the children in their care.
>
> You have to look at individual circumstances, the child's family and the environment in which they live to understand the child's needs. Sometimes that means getting external agencies to help them. But having that dialogue with families is absolutely vital if their child is to get on.
>
> (Gareth Morewood, Priestnall School, Telephone interview, March 9, 2018)

Morewood sees his role as an advocate for the child and their family. It is time-consuming, he admits, but their individual circumstances have to be set out against the outcomes the school wants the child to achieve. Priestnall prides itself on turning out a very low proportion of pupils who are not in education, employment or training (NEET) each year, with clear pathways into adulthood for all learners.

> When you build a relationship with a family you have to be more fluid in your approach. It might mean getting to know them early on and going to their home for a visit.
>
> Investing in good personal relationships early on means you work more effectively down the line and is a good foundation for a co-produced relationship. The children also need to see the school and parents working closely together.

This process also gives parents the skills and capability to keep on top of things themselves. By Year 10, it may be enough for Morewood to keep in touch with families via e-mail because the

(*continued*)

## Priestnall School case study (*continued*)

relationship and understanding between the home and school will have been so well-established already.

The school's strong relationships with parents are based on mutual trust and respect and listening to the views and concerns of the other. Morewood says it is important for schools to deliver what they say they will, or to explain why it might not be possible. Parents should never be backed into a corner or feel under pressure to accept a strategy they believe to be wrong for their child, but be given options and jointly-agreed outcomes.

At the time of writing, Priestnall had 54 pupils on roll with EHCPs including children with disabilities, medical needs and complex learning difficulties that might require personal care. While the proportion is in line with national norms, the severity of need among the pupils makes the school unusual.

Among the many strategies employed by Morewood at Priestnall are early dialogues with families whose children are in Years 4 and 5. Parents and carers are invited into school to get a feel for it and so it becomes familiar. Some families are visited at home, with regular discussions taking place subsequently face to face, or by e-mail.

"The management of communication between the school and home is key to these relationships," he says.

> You begin with a conversation by telephone but then follow it up after a few days with a face to face meeting to decide outcomes and suggest what strategies we can use. We ask the parent to discuss proposals with their child – it reduces the anxiety on the child if the parents tell them – and then get them to report back.
>
> In this way, we are arming parents with positives and giving them the basis for a working partnership.

## The other side of the Priestnall story – a parents' perspective

Debby Elley's twin 14-year-old sons have autism, and one of them, Bobby, now attends Priestnall. She says she is one of the lucky ones to have had generally good relationships with all the schools her sons have attended.

> Teachers sometimes feel they have to pretend that they know it all but that isn't what parents want. We want teachers who are willing to listen, to draw on our knowledge as the parent of this child and to learn from what happens at home.
>
> The most annoying thing that teachers can say is 'oh don't worry, we've had a child with autism here before.' It's a bit like saying I have a friend with red hair and thinking they can sing like Ed Sheeran.
>
> You may well have had a child with autism before, but it was not my child.

Elley believes a culture of inclusion and positivity, led by the school, is vital if a child with special needs is to go in to school happy and willing to learn. This is exactly what she found at Priestnall.

> After my first meeting with Gareth I knew the school understood what it was doing and felt confident that Bobby would be properly looked after. The teachers had been trained in autism, and when I went to the parents' evening for the first time I felt like a normal parent because they already understood my child. We were able to talk about Bobby taking his autism into account and there were things that didn't need to be said about this, because they knew and understood him.

When necessary, staff at Priestnall have adapted their practice to accommodate Bobby's challenges. For example, a history teacher interviewed Bobby about a project he was working on about women's rights, because he wasn't able to write down his thoughts and knowledge with clarity.

In Year 7 in PE, a teacher gave Bobby a tennis racket during rounders so that he would have a better chance of hitting the ball. What makes Priestnall really special, Elley says, is that none of the other children would have blinked an eyelid at this, because they've had peer training in autism.

"The teachers are guided by the curriculum support team, which has kudos within the school and they are listened to by the staff, and not seen as a nuisance" Elley adds

> As a parent this is very reassuring, because your child is accepted like every other pupil.
>
> If you want to be listened to as a parent you have to tell them when things are going right, as well as when they're going wrong. That way they are more likely to listen. So, I always write to the school to thank them for the good things they are doing. When they go wrong, I am inclined to think 'big deal' – everyone makes mistakes at times.
>
> The home and school are constantly passing the baton, and you have to have consistency in your approach. If Bobby is having a bad morning, I will e-mail the school and forewarn them that there might be an explosion today. It's not a case of kicking him out of the front door with a sigh of relief, and passing him on hoping he has a good day, but having some respect for the teachers who will have to deal with it
>
> There has to be mutual respect and understanding, and an acknowledgement that we all want what is best for the child. Getting defensive doesn't work. Gareth knows I support the school 100% and that if they end up trying something a bit different with Bobby, it is always through working jointly with me.

This level of collaboration has come into its own in the past year, with Bobby choosing his GCSE options. The school has allowed him to focus on subjects that will help him achieve his dream of a career in computing. Elley said the school listened to her concerns about forcing

Bobby down a highly academic path that would not have led to success or engaged his interests.

The school also brings in a peer group trainer, who has encouraged Bobby's classmates to imagine what it would be like to have autism and holds assemblies about special needs. As a result, pupils at Priestnall understand the communication barriers and have become advocates for pupils like Bobby.

"He has never been bullied as a result of these interventions. If your peer group understands the problems, then they cease to be an issue. Bobby is free to learn because the barriers have been broken down."

## Top tips

- Identify and have purpose in what you are trying to do from an external face and have a policy on your philosophy of engagement and what you are seeking to achieve.
- Start the process of engagement as early as possible, with feeder primary teachers and parents you know are coming up to the school. Early meetings will help to build those relationships.
- Be humble in the way you engage with people, and don't assume you know all the answers. No-one has a monopoly on how to handle every situation.
- Listen to what parents are telling you. They have known the child from birth and will have their own strategies for dealing with difficulties.
- Be flexible. If you can't agree with the parents on a strategy for their child, offer to give it a go for a couple of weeks to see if it will work. Undertake to reconsider this course of action if it doesn't go as planned.
- Give people options and do not back them into a corner.
- Plan ahead but always review what you are doing to ensure that it has worked or continues to work.
- Encourage a culture that working in partnership is a strength, and this will have more impact.

- Keep in regular contact with parents using all available means, including face to face meetings, e-mail and text messaging.
- Establish trust and maintain trust by delivering what you have promised to do. If you have told parents that something can be done, then do it.
- Never give false hope. Be honest and realistic about what can be achieved and put it in writing to the young person and the family, if appropriate.

DL

## Notes

1 https://assets.publishing.service.gov.uk/government/uploads/system/uploads/attachment_data/file/552342/SFR20_2016_Main_Text.pdf
2 https://gov.wales/docs/statistics/2017/170726-school-census-results-2017-en.pdf
3 www.gov.scot/Topics/Statistics/Browse/School-Education/Summarystatsforschools
4 www.education-ni.gov.uk/sites/default/files/publications/education/Special%20educational%20%20needs%202017-18.pdf
5 www.legislation.gov.uk/ukpga/2014/6/contents/enacted
6 www.parentsinneed.org/
7 www.hanen.org/Home.aspx

# 8 Setting up a new school

In the coming decade hundreds, if not thousands, of new schools will need to be built in the UK to accommodate around half a million additional pupils going through the education system[1] according to pupil number projections to 2027.

Since 2010, the government's preferred way of opening new schools has been through the Free Schools policy, which enabled interested groups such as parents, teachers, educational charities and others to open schools that were state-funded but independent from local authority control.

More recently, local authorities have been allowed to establish new schools through the presumption route,[2] meaning they have to identify the need for a new school to create additional places. Having specified the type of school they want, they instigate a competition process for proposers to come forward to set up the school.

Local authorities, which retain responsibilities for school admissions, would prefer to be more in control of the process and given the funding to set up schools as, when and where required.[3]

The need for additional places does not preclude the opening of new schools for other reasons. The New Schools Network, the organisation set up by the government to oversee the expansion of the Free Schools programme and which currently has more than 300 schools in the pipeline, is targeting the creation of new schools in areas of educational underperformance. The idea is that the new schools will offer a higher standard of learning than existing ones in those communities.

But regardless of the processes involved, opening a new school presents prospective heads and governors with new opportunities relating to the vision and ethos of the school, and challenges in attracting pupils.

Why would parents take a leap of faith in committing to a school with no Ofsted reports, no SATs or GCSE results and no reputation in the locality?

Mark Lehain, former Interim Director of New Schools Network (now Director of Parents & Teachers for Excellence) and the founder of the Bedford Free School in 2011, one of the first free schools set up under the policy, has used his own experience to advise others.

He recalls 'an awful lot of problems' and confusion as the local authority objected to the proposals for the Bedford Free School, while the founders of the school tried to reassure parents who were interested in their children attending that it was going to go ahead.

> Communication was vitally important at this time. The first thing we did was to appoint a leadership team. A few weeks later we appointed the first five or six teachers and held a teachers' evening where parents who were interested could come and meet them. Some of the staff were in local schools and may have been known to some of the parents already, but others came from further afield.
>
> We held meetings in the buildings that were intended to house the new school but once work began to refurbish, we moved to other locations, occasionally going out to the community. This showed respect to those who were interested in the school and made it easier for people to come along if they lived locally.
>
> We wanted to attract a comprehensive intake and we figured middle-class parents would find us regardless, so we wanted to attract those from other areas where finding out about the new school might have been more difficult.
>
> (Mark Lehain, Telephone interview, August 9, 2018)

Lehain says asking people to sign up to a new school was challenging:

> You must justify the need for a new school to them and ideally you want this to travel by word of mouth. But getting people to come

> to meetings and events was important because they attracted others to come along, who then spread the word that they had attended, and had seen other people they knew.
>
> We built up confidence in the new school in this way, so that people didn't feel out on a limb by being in a meeting where there was no-one they knew. We started to home in on this and got parents to bring friends with them to find out if they were interested. This worked well for us.
>
> I also gave out my mobile number, which meant people could call me if they had a question. As a figurehead of a new school, you have to make yourself available.

He recalls the most commonly asked questions among prospective parents: Will it be a strict school? Will you have a smart uniform? What will you do about bullying? Will behaviour be good at the school?

Then came the supplementary questions among those who were following the progress of the opening schedule: What if you don't get planning permission? Will the buildings be ready on time?

> These were very understandable questions and we have to answer them honestly. If we didn't know the answer, then we told them we didn't know. You must be upfront. I told them I expected the buildings to be finished, but if they weren't, then we would have a contingency plan.
>
> We showed families the uniform early on because we had some samples, and during the consultation evening a couple of prospective pupils put them on and photos were taken. Those were then used extensively in promotional materials. Seeing children wearing the school blazer suddenly made it very real. It was a defining moment.

NSN advises new schools to consult with parents as widely as possible, but to be clear where the boundaries are, and what is not open to change.

"You must be mindful that you can't make everyone happy, so you have to be very clear about what your expectations are as people may interpret them differently," Lehain says.

> Interestingly a few people thought a free school meant that you were free to come in or not, and it turned out that quite a few pupils who were among the first intake had not been regular attenders in other schools. It came as a shock to some parents that we expected them to be there every day.
>
> So, you must be clear, but humble, and let parents decide whether this is the right school for their child, and don't deviate from the offer. Every new school is a blank canvas and people will have their own view of what it should be.
>
> I made it as clear as I could that we would have high expectations of attendance and behaviour and effort. Behaviour included coming into and leaving school every day. The most successful schools are those that are clear about their policies, ethos and vision.

## Top tips for attracting parents to a brand-new school

- Make sure you have a figurehead in place early on, as that person will become the spokesperson for the school in the early days.
- Make yourself visible and always available to parents when they want to speak to you.
- Make clear what your vision is so people can decide whether to buy into it, and be firm in sticking to it.
- Be aware of local issues and challenges facing the community you're seeking to serve.
- Consult with parents and families on the things you can deliver. Don't ask for their feedback on the new school uniform if you've already chosen the colours and design.
- Ensure your vision and ethos have children and young people at the centre.

The following three case studies outline the different circumstances and approaches taken in opening schools from scratch.

## Case study 1: The Reach Academy, Feltham

In setting up The Reach Academy, in Feltham, west London, seven years ago, Ed Vainker had a vision in mind. That was to create a school in an area where new places were needed locally, and in which children from all backgrounds could thrive and flourish:

> Three of us founded this school and two had worked in secondary schools in London serving vulnerable communities. In every case, these schools were large and quite impersonal, and it was hard for some pupils to receive the levels of support and encouragement they needed.
>
> Transition from primary to secondary was also a problem, so we wanted to make that easier. But at the heart of it all was family engagement, and this is what we are invested in. Our priority was always to secure advantage for our pupils through continuity of relationships and the academic offer.
>
> (Ed Vainker, Reach Academy, April 26, 2018)

To that end, the Reach Academy opened as an all-through free school for two to 18 year-olds in 2011, having gained approval from the Department for Education the previous year, with just a reception class and Year 7. In the academic year 2018–2019 it will be full and at capacity for the first time. It is at this stage, as far as Vainker is concerned, that it can begin properly to make its mark.

> Now we will know all the pupils, their families and there be continuity across the curriculum because children won't be arriving into the secondary from 20 different feeder schools.

(*continued*)

**Case study 1: The Reach Academy, Feltham (*continued*)**

> The history teacher, for example, won't be teaching old material to some pupils because they've covered it previously in their primary school. At the point I expect the academic advantage of our school to start having an impact.

The ability to sustain high quality relationships with families was among the key aspects of setting up the Reach Academy:

> Feltham is a very mixed area and as in all communities, there are children who are vulnerable, and with parents whose own experience of school was not necessarily positive. It was important to us that they felt this school was going to be different and that their children could be successful here.
>
> We believe that schools have a vital role to play in the community, and that includes the quality of relationships. We can be strong on this aspect of our work, and be academically rigorous, because it is not a case of one or the other. The success of the pupils and their ability to thrive is dependent on these relationships.

Recruitment to the new school was done largely through word of mouth with Vainker and his team visiting people in their homes for a cup of tea, holding meetings in local community centres and giving out fliers in the street. At this stage, the school didn't have a building so there was nothing to show that was tangible other than words and good intentions.

> For many parents it was a complete leap of faith and they were, literally, committing to me and my deputy because there was nothing else. There was no pre-existing reputation, or Ofsted inspection or exam results to refer to. We weren't

(*continued*)

## Case study 1: The Reach Academy, Feltham (*continued*)

> part of an academy trust or coming out of a church or other community organisation that was known locally. We were an unknown quantity and that was challenging.

Among the first and most important appointments made at the school at the outset was that of Kay Stone, the family support officer. No matter how tight the school's budget may be at any point in the future, Vainker states emphatically, her role will never be in danger.

Stone comes from the local community and relates to those living in it. Initially appointed as a teaching assistant, she was soon moved to the family support role, a job that was created for her. She runs parenting courses, carries out home visits and helps parents with tasks such as form-filling or applying for benefits support.

She says the parenting classes are designed to improve relationships between carers and their children:

> I'm not here to judge parents but to show them that by changing one aspect of their approach it may make things better.
>
> I love seeing that eureka moment when a parent realises it might be the way they are dealing with a situation that is the problem, and not something wrong with their child. There is a fine line to be walked between being helpful and supportive, and intrusive in their family life.
>
> Now, if they are struggling, they know where to come for help and just knowing someone cares can be a huge help. For some, parenting is a very lonely experience and just getting up in the morning can be a huge challenge. But knowing the school is supportive can make a difference.

Parents were involved, as far as possible, in the early decision-making relating to the new school.

(*continued*)

### Case study 1: The Reach Academy, Feltham (*continued*)

Vainker says:

> We were very clear about how we wanted the school to be, and we consulted on issues where we felt we could genuinely act on their feedback – so, for example, we asked for their thoughts on the uniform, the extra-curricular offer and wrap-around care.
>
> We were also very clear about the non-negotiables. For example, pupils are not allowed to bring packed lunches and must have a school meal. We think this is an important part of the day and a chance for pupils and teachers to have a shared experience eating together. Packed lunches can be nutritionally questionable. Some parents said: 'but my child is a fussy eater, so we won't send to the school in that case'. We said ok, that's your choice, but this is how we are.

Each new family was, and still is, visited at home before the child starts at Reach. Normally two members of staff attend, with one talking to the child and the other to the parents or carers.

> It is good to see the child in their own environment and to understand their interests and how they live at home. It is a neutral place where we give families our handbook that sets out the school's policies, what shoes are acceptable as part of the uniform, and so on. Families know there is no hiding the ball. There are no hidden expectations and we do not ask the children to be something we haven't taught them to be.

It is also chance for the staff to find out about parental employment, their housing situation, if there are any siblings and even whether they'd be willing to work at the school in any capacity.

(*continued*)

## Case study 1: The Reach Academy, Feltham (*continued*)

Children joining the secondary school in Year 7 attend summer school before the start of term, where they learn how to be a successful Reach pupil and find out what equipment they are expected to have and how to move around the school. "We introduce them to our values, so they understand what they are, and they do a short English and maths assessment," Vainker says.

"It is also another chance to talk to their parents about their child and to ensure, for example, that they are on the special needs register if they need to be and any other needs they have are being met."

All teachers at Reach have a mobile phone provided by the school on which parents and pupils can call them, though Vainker says they are rarely contacted outside of school hours. "If there happen to be lots of questions about a piece of homework then that tells the teacher they may need to review how they set that piece of work." As head teacher, he receives an average of two calls a week from parents inquiring about some aspect or other of school life.

Future plans for the school include the opening of a community 'hub' which will house health professionals such as midwives, health visitors and a GP, and a citizen's advice office, amongst others. It will also offer adult education and parenting courses. It means that a local mother-to-be, on finding out she is pregnant, will have her first consultation with the midwife on the school site, laying the foundations for her child's future involvement with the school.

> All of this is a lot of hard work, admittedly, but we see it as an investment. We were able to lay down certain parameters because we started the school from scratch, and this is what we have chosen to prioritise. We employed Kay when we had just 100 children at the school and compromised on other roles.

(*continued*)

## Case study 1: The Reach Academy, Feltham (*continued*)

This is a good school and we believe that the focus on relationships is a key lever in making it so and achieving the outcomes we want. Staff spend a lot of time here on relationships than they might in other schools, and that might mean less time marking or planning but that is a compromise we're happy with.

In the end teachers are freer to teach because of staff members like Kay, but in helping a parent in difficulty they are also directly contributing to that child being more likely to come into school regularly and being successful. You could wait for things to unravel for that child, or you can get in front of the problem and offer support as early as possible.

## Case study 2: Bure Park Primary School, Oxfordshire

Bure Park Primary School sprang up on a patch of former farmland in the year 2000. Around it, developers were building a housing estate of several hundred homes to cater for this growing market town in Oxfordshire.

With its excellent links by road and train to London, Birmingham and the south-west of England, Bicester was rapidly becoming a commuter town with cheaper house prices than in the capital, and a more rural, close community feel than a sprawling conurbation like the West Midlands. Both were within an hour commute, with Oxford just 15 miles away.

"We were being built as a community school, but actually there was no community here," Yvonne Hewson, the head teacher

(*continued*)

## Case study 2: Bure Park Primary School, Oxfordshire (*continued*)

explains. "There were no 'local' families. People were coming here to live from London, Birmingham, Manchester – everywhere – because of its location and affordable house prices."

Hewson was one of a small number of staff appointed to open the school, many of whom were still serving notice on existing jobs, while trying to set up Bure Park at the same time.

When it eventually opened the school had 69 pupils of all ages, scattered in every class. Today, it has almost 500, and has been heavily oversubscribed in recent years.

"The local children we admitted came from other schools in the town were what was known as 'fresh starters.' They hadn't got on in their previous primaries, and those schools were happy for us to take them in."

The local population had some concerns about the expansion of the town. Bure Park was built on green land which was being taken away. "There used to be an annual bonfire display on this site, so there were people who weren't happy with the changes," Hewson says.

"But it was the lack of community that was among our biggest problems. We never knew who was going to move in to the houses that were being built and sold, so we were never aware exactly how many children were going to come and how much funding we would get. It was very difficult to plan ahead."

A team of staff, led by designated head teacher Rob Pearson, began to get the word out that a new school was opening. Because Bure Park was being built to serve a housing estate with a specific catchment area there were, at least, no objections to it from other schools in the town.

"We lost some children from the estate early on because the school hadn't yet opened, and the parents had to place them

(*continued*)

## Case study 2: Bure Park Primary School, Oxfordshire (*continued*)

somewhere else and couldn't really wait. When we opened we had few pupils in every class, and some year groups were merged because there weren't enough children."

Parents were drawn to the school through leaflet drops locally and by holding public meetings:

> We talked a lot about our philosophy and we referred to it a "A New School for a New Millennium," so parents understood that we had innovative ideas about the school day, the curriculum and teaching.
>
> One of the other primary schools kindly allowed us to open a small office on its site. They didn't mind, as we weren't going to attract their intake and they were far enough away for us to have no negative impact on them. This gave us somewhere people could come to talk to the head and the school administrator, who ran an 'open door' policy.
>
> (Yvonne Hewson and Karen Ward, Bure Park Primary, July 5, 2018)

Community life was built up by inviting groups to use the still-empty classrooms. A playgroup was set up and coffee mornings held. In the absence of any other meeting place on the estate, the school became a focal point where parents and toddlers could gather and get to know their new neighbours.

"We had visitors constantly and we would show anyone around who wanted to see the school," Hewson says.

> There are shops and other local businesses, a pub and church here now, but at the time there was nowhere else to go but

(*continued*)

## Case study 2: Bure Park Primary School, Oxfordshire (*continued*)

the school. No-one knew anyone else here, so the school became a meeting place.

Parents were encouraged to come in as reading helpers and we had a barbecue that first year, which has become a tradition that goes on to this day. Similarly, we had 'sharing assembles' where the pupils would show their work to parents, because this would bring families together. These assemblies also still happen.

Bure Park's first Ofsted inspection in 2001 found it to be a good school, which attracted more interest.

We didn't just want families to look at the curriculum, but the fact this was a caring school with a vibrant and exciting curriculum and our aim was to turn out rounded children who were ready for life, and not just for the next phase in their education.

When you are the new kid on the block, word soon gets out and everyone wants to know what you are doing.

## Case study 3: Boulevard Academy School, Hull

Boulevard Academy School opened in 2013 to meet the need for a 'good school' in an area of Hull that had been left behind with a declining fishing industry.

"Hull had been languishing at the bottom of league tables for years and three philanthropists, including local business people,

(*continued*)

## Case study 3: Boulevard Academy School, Hull (*continued*)

stepped in to open a new school," explains Andy Grace, the Principal. "It was an area of high crime, low aspirations and poor standards of literacy and numeracy.

"We wanted to secure academic outcomes for young people, whether it be university or apprenticeships, in an area where jobs are transient and often accompanied by the question 'would you like fries with that?'"

While local MPs had supported the creation of free schools in the city, the local authority was less keen. With just months to go before the school was due to open, Grace discovered that Boulevard had not been included as an option in the list of schools drawn up for parents applying for secondary places for their children.

"There was no obligation for the local authority to inform people that a school was opening, but our problem was that we needed to get a significant number through the door to make the school viable."

Grace found himself quickly becoming the public face and embodiment of the future free school, and the visionary of what it was to become.

He set up a hot-desk in a community centre to make himself available to meet interested parents, and 'piggy-backed' on local networks. From his own pocket, Grace paid for the printing of 25,000 leaflets advertising the new school and distributed them to home and the locality. A supporter of the school managed to secure a discount for printing costs, so the outlay for the leaflets came to £200.

"On one occasion I turned up at a local councillor's surgery as this gave me access to local parents, and I even muscled in on parents' evenings at primary schools. Sometimes I'd invite myself

(*continued*)

## Case study 3: Boulevard Academy School, Hull (*continued*)

to attend, but I also hung around in the car park to talk to them and hand out leaflets," he says.

During one primary school Christmas fayre, he set up a pasting table to hand out leaflets and information to promote interest and attract possible recruits. "We'd turn up pretty much anywhere there was a community gathering," Grace says.

> After a while I started bumping into the same parents for a second or third time, and they become disciples for the new school within their communities. They would mention the proposed school to others and promote what we were trying to do. Sometimes, I'd get invited to meet interested families in their own homes, or in local cafes. It became an organic process of getting the messages out.
>
> Local businesses such as fish and chip shops and local convenience stores would also carry our leaflets to distribute to customers. Gradually, we were getting the word out.
>
> There was no money for advertising, but Hull (rugby league) Football Club were helpful as the new school was to be built on their old ground. They used the big screens in their new ground (shared with Hill City FC) to advertise the new academy.
>
> (Andy Grace, Boulevard Academy, Telephone interview, July 11, 2018)

Grace gave his mobile phone number to parents who expressed an interest in sending their children to Boulevard, so they could contact him whenever they wanted to – a practice he has maintained to this day. "If you want their support you have to make yourself available to them," he says.

(*continued*)

## Case study 3: Boulevard Academy School, Hull (*continued*)

As he met and talked to more people, it became apparent that parents wanted a good local school that would be part of their locality. Conversations included grandparents, who had often themselves left school at the age of 14 to work on the trawlers knowing they had a job for life.

> Those grandparents thought that their children would have the same job security, so education wasn't necessarily a priority. But those children, who are now parents, have not always worked as the jobs have gone, and they want better for their children. In discussions, we emphasised that we wanted the same as they did and to secure outcomes that would lead to jobs for their children, and therefore a more secure future for the parents in their old age.
>
> We were always careful not to dumb down the messages we tried to get across and to be mindful of our audience. Families appreciated the straight-talking approach and wanted someone to listen, as well as to talk to them. It wasn't enough to ask them to trust us. We had to be seen to be doing the right thing and to give them some ownership of what the school was going to be about.

Some children were pushed in the direction of Boulevard because other schools were oversubscribed. Grace admits he once stood and waited for parents coming out of appeals hearings to get their children into other schools. "While wishing them well in getting a place at their chosen school, I handed them a leaflet for Boulevard and asked them to consider it as an option if things didn't work out," he says.

(*continued*)

**Case study 3: Boulevard Academy School, Hull (*continued*)**

"We had some concerns that we'd end up with parents who really didn't want their children to be here, or who hadn't bothered to apply to any school and came by default. It was important for us that the people who came to Boulevard brought into our ethos and thinking and understood what we were trying to do."

The school courted controversy locally with its long school day, and shorter holidays, with the summer break lasting only for the month of August. But it means that, over the course of five years, students attending Boulevard get about ayear's worth of extra lesson time.

Pupils do their homework at school because parents are not always able to provide the appropriate facilities for study. It also ensures that children who have no internet access at home don't miss out.

"Our USP now as a school is the extent to which we work closely to parents, but we worked hard to create these opportunities."

## Further reading

www.gov.uk/set-up-free-school
www.newschoolsnetwork.org/

DL

## Notes

1 https://assets.publishing.service.gov.uk/government/uploads/system/uploads/attachment_data/file/723851/2018Release_Projections_Text.pdf
2 https://assets.publishing.service.gov.uk/government/uploads/system/uploads/attachment_data/file/706171/Academy_and_free_school_presumption_departmental_advice.pdf
3 www.local.gov.uk/about/news/lga-responds-dfe-announcement-school-places

# 9 Media

## Introduction

We live in a media-saturated age where every aspect of public – and, in many cases, private – life is open to broadcast and publication.

Publicity for your school used to mean a quick phone call or e-mail to the local paper or radio station to send along a reporter to record a sports day, sponsored walk or prize-winning pupils.

Today, however, it can often seem as if making a video to 'go viral' is the very least a school must do to get itself noticed.

The flipside of that, of course, is that when something bad happens, controlling the message becomes an almost impossible challenge as Facebook posts, tweets and WhatsApp group messages multiply in minutes and cannot be checked for accuracy.

On top of that, local papers have replaced specialist education reporters – with whom a school could once build a relationship – with content writers operating across a wide range of subjects and feeding more than one publication.

This makes it harder for schools forge the kind of links that would have been natural in the past, though many still try.

It has, however, never been easier for schools to set up their own direct channels of communication and effectively be their own media outlet, from the traditional weekly school newsletter now converted to e-mail or podcast to the website video channel or the Facebook page with daily school news.

The media's commitment to engaging readers and giving everyone a voice by inviting comments online can also work against schools when inaccurate or unpleasant contributions are posted beneath a story.

Media organisations have a responsibility to moderate reader comments but, they would argue, have to draw a fine line between curbing the less-pleasant impulses of their readers and protecting their right to free speech.

Schools are also increasingly the target of Freedom of Information (FoI) requests from the media on everything from their provision – or lack of it – of gender-neutral toilets and changing rooms to taxi bills incurred by senior management and questionable relationships with uniform suppliers.

Managing the media with parents in mind – whether trouble-shooting or seeking positive PR – requires some understanding of how it all works. In this chapter, we have asked a range of voices for their thoughts on what a school should and shouldn't do to get the best out of the media, how to avoid a bad news story damaging its reputation permanently and the steps schools can take to make sure they stay on the front foot when it comes to managing social media.

They include editors and reporters on local and national media, public relations and marketing specialists, school leaders and governors and parents. And they don't all take the same line on dealing with the media, by any means.

## John Dexter, parent, former deputy head of Trinity RC School, Nottingham, now education director, Nottingham city council

If parents want to have a whine and a moan, they sometimes hit you with the old 'we're going to go to the press.' It's something senior leaders will experience more than new teachers, but it could happen to any member of staff and it is bound to bother you.

Although, in my experience, they seldom follow through on it, the press must give you the right to reply should they do so.

The press is an important conduit for information to parents and the wider community and it can shape parents' perception of the school, so it's important that the school leadership – or a key person – has a relationship with the media.

One way to build it is to invite the media into your school to have a look around, meet a few people, such as students and parent-governors, or to a special event which showcases your school, like the prize-giving and drama evening, which parents love to see reported. This includes reporters and editors, if you can, and talk to them about the things they'd be interested in and follow that up with little stories via e-mail.

One of the things that has annoyed me about local media is the comments that are added to the bottom of a story that has been published online. One local news site once ran a story about a parent who didn't get their child into a school and was also turned down on appeal.

The parent was quoted as blaming 'all these families coming from abroad' which triggered a stream of racist comments beneath the story. In the end, I rang the editor and asked him to take it down, which he did. It needed someone to ring but it's important to monitor the press generally and to see what stories are going out about your school and if parents are involved and to decide if – or how – you are going to react. Sometimes it is better to make 'no comment' and all of us need to remember there are often two sides to a story.

If you're an newly qualified teacher (NQT) or still inexperienced, and something serious like a racist incident arises, flag it up to your senior leader and don't feel you have to handle the press yourself. If it's something lower level on Twitter or Facebook that's annoying rather than law-breaking, then my advice is don't engage.

For example, when there were stories in the press about the rate of exclusions in schools, I saw a tweet claiming Nottingham schools weren't 'allowed' to exclude pupils. It was utter nonsense, but it would also have been pointless to engage because – as an educator – you risk giving the story more attention.

I recommend all teachers – new recruits, in particular – to think hard about their social media activity; I would advise them not to 'follow' parents online, let alone pupils.

I was never on Facebook when I was a teacher, but we did have instances of staff – through ignorance – getting into trouble. One teacher emerged from a particularly trying day and posted on his

Facebook account, 'that year 9, what a bunch' which a colleague fortunately spotted before a parent did.

It's a question of the professional approach versus the personal and what was acceptable when you were a student is not acceptable for parents and pupils to see now you are a professional. Schools have policies so teachers should read them, but also ask about social media and how the school views pupils using it, teachers using it and the approach with the official school accounts, too.

The other aspect of social media is the speed at which news travels around the community.

A child once came up to me at school and said he and others had read on Facebook that one of the pupils had died but I knew nothing about it. It turned out to be true, but it took me a few hours to confirm the details, a very tense experience in itself.

Eventually, it was confirmed by the local hospital. In a scenario like that, younger, more inexperienced staff might be tempted to post a message of condolence online with #RIP because that's come to be the norm.

Again, it's best avoided until the senior leadership has confirmed it and even then, it may be seen as inappropriate because parents might see it as a semi-official view from the school.

I think you definitely have to step away from how you'd behave personally and simply have a conversation, talk, discuss and involve senior colleagues, and, guess what, you will learn!

## Stephanie Sparrow, parent, national education writer

Head teachers need a clear strategy on how to deal with the media and to share it with parents via the school website. It might be, for example, that they only respond to media requests if they were about serious and immediate matters such as a safety issue, [a] missing child or the impact of a tragedy.

There needs to be a single point of contact – a member of the senior leadership team, if not the head, though I think that if there is a serious incident such as a death, most parents expect the head teacher to be the one giving a clear statement across all the school's media channels.

The single voice is particularly important if a school is the focus of or caught up in a national story where the media descends en masse.

Schools and colleges in my area – the north-west – they were besieged by international media in the aftermath of the attack on Manchester Arena in May 2017. Many students or their siblings had been affected or were distressed. School and college leaders had to support frightened pupils, manage their own emotions, and deal with the shock and grief of the community, while investigating unexplained absences and fending off calls from journalists. . . .

Generally, there are some basic, practical things that can get overlooked when dealing with the media. If parents have signed a consent form for the use of photos, for example, this still needs to be updated regularly to allow for changes in circumstances. One parent may not be allowed access to the children or even, in extreme cases, know where the children are at school, for example.

By allowing a child's photograph to appear in a news story online or in print, schools can unwittingly reveal children's locations.

As a journalist, I do think there's a danger that people responsible for marketing in schools are so keen to attract publicity that they sometimes create banal press releases, websites posts or tweet about everyday achievements. Should they really be tweeting: "Year 3 is getting reacquainted with multiplication," together with a shot of bored-looking pupils? And surely children have a right to learn their multiplication undisturbed?

But, on the other hand, openness and regular communication with parents should be welcomed. We sometimes forget that it hasn't always been so.

## Nick Bannister, national PR consultant and parent

If a school receives negative press in the media, there are various steps it can take to minimise [the] damage to its reputation.

It shouldn't hide from the press and hope that it will 'go away' as that would simply prompt speculation and rumours. It should give a clear and positive response to the situation, acknowledging concern and setting out the positive measures that will be undertaken.

Internal communications procedures really do need to be sharp so if there is negative press, so your response should fall into place. Don't wait until the time you receive negative press – prepare for it.

For example, you need to have in place a process that mean that pupils, staff, parents and community and other stakeholders are reassured about the how the school is going to deal with an issue before they read or see it in the media.

If there is a story that has the potential to become a row – a parent with a grievance about a school policy, for example – it is best to try and contact the complainant to agree [to] a solution or at least a way forward. This may well avoid fanning the flames of an argument in the press.

Make sure that, with any response to the media, your message remains simple and clear. Ideally, put forward one clear message or, at the very most, three. The more complex and nuanced your response the more diluted it becomes in the media.

Schools can't really rely on local authority press offices in the way they used to – local authorities have taken massive hits to their budgets over the past few years and this has affected the resources they can dedicate to their press offices.

But many schools do maintain an agreement with their local authority to provide crisis PR management, or buy in their services on an 'as-needed' basis.

I've spoken to heads who have taken this approach and they have found it very effective. One head in the south-west bought the services of his local authority press office when his school became a national news story and the press team acted as the interface between school and media, preparing press statements and advising on media handling.

The head said:

> Our approach was to be as accommodating as possible to the media but even then we still had reporters outside the school gates trying

> to talk to the kids. We were very firm with the press that if they were to come on site that had to be at our invitation.
>
> We also briefed students about the fact that this situation had caused a lot of trauma for many of our students. If they were approached by the media they were to let us, with press office support, deal with it.
>
> (Nick Bannister, national PR consultant, July 2018)

Positive media coverage is increasingly important as schools compete for pupils.

Over time, a positive presence in the media can put your school at the forefront of parents' minds. Schools are much more than an Ofsted rating or a league table position, and PR enables them to present a fuller picture of what it is that makes them a vibrant and successful place.

PR can also help schools in their efforts to generate income from their facilities, such as room lettings and sports facilities while maintaining a positive profile is vital for schools that have been through a rough patch, such as a bad Ofsted judgement.

## Tracy Powell, parent, BA journalism leader, Nottingham Trent University and former newspaper editor

In the media industry it's a common-known fact that the best PR tip for anyone, business, school or public service, experiencing negative publicity of any kind is not to ignore it. I have experienced first-hand, both as a parent and a newspaper editor, organisations 'burying their heads in the sand' and failing to acknowledge publicly that something negative has happened. The problem with this approach is that it can cause mistrust, anger and lack of respect for the organisation concerned, and often leads to parents, clients or customers voting with their feet.

An example: as a parent some years ago, an incident occurred at my daughters' school involving inappropriate behaviour of a male teacher towards female students. My daughters appeared to have some knowledge of what had happened via the 'rumour mill,' however as parents we didn't get an official statement from the school. This led to much bad feeling among parents who felt the school was trying to hide something bad. We wanted to know what had happened. In my opinion, this feeling of mistrust and lack of respect for the school we had over this incident could have been avoided had the school put out a statement telling us the basics. Of course, if criminal charges against someone have been brought, this information may be limited. But it is always better to say something rather than not commenting at all.

The same can be said when dealing with the press. Often journalists and editors will have unconfirmed information about an incident, or even 'off the record' details of something that has happened, but if the organisation fails to issue any kind of statement, sometimes little can be reported. This could be something that is in the public interest to be aware of. In a school for example, it may be that there has been an outbreak of an illness that other schools and parents should be aware of, or it may be that there has been a serious incident involving some pupils.

Always better to be honest, and let people know what is going on. You will be respected and trusted more for it.

## Dealing with the local press

- Have a single point of contact in the school for media enquiries.
- In a crisis, parents will expect to hear from the head.
- Forge a relationship, ideally with the editor. It doesn't mean you will avoid bad publicity if your school is involved in a negative news story, but if they know who to come to for a comment, you will have your side of the story out there more quickly.
- Local papers are incredibly short-staffed. Anything that you can do to make their life easier – feeding them good stories with images and, ideally, video, where appropriate – will be welcome. They have space to fill on websites and social media platforms and they need a steady stream of fresh content to maintain click rates and please advertisers.

## To comment or not to comment?

Schools are under no obligation to comment to the media on any story, but, in practice, the need to communicate with parents and retain their trust may transcend any desire to keep quiet and hope a bad story on a local news website or in the paper will lose momentum. The pitfalls with 'no comment' are that rumour, speculation and misinformation fill the vacuum.

When the story is serious enough to attract the attention of the national media, should the same apply? Giving a quote, putting out a statement, even employing the services of professional PR people – if the money is there! – to handle a crisis situation such as a claim of inappropriate behaviour by a member of staff or a scandal of some kind which the community is up in arms about can give a school and staff a sense of taking control, but one national journalist with many years of experience of working for the press, says that it may not be necessary.

> I would question the advice that it is always better to talk to the media than not. There are cases where media lawyers will be unwilling to run a story unless the writer has talked to the school concerned. If the writer can get to the head or chair of governors then they have at least put the allegation to them and a no comment will suffice for the purposes of publishing, whereas if they don't manage to speak to anyone they have a problem. Nowadays it's possible to send an email and check if it has been read, however, but you still have to prove [that] the right person read it.
>
> (Tracy Powell, BA Journalism course leader, Nottingham Trent University, August 2018)

## Using social media positively

Sophie Turner is marketing manager at Nottingham High School, an independent fee-paying school for boys and girls in Nottingham:

> Make sure that issues of safeguarding and privacy are considered when using social media. Parental consent is legally required for schools to be able to post photographs of children, and even with that in place children's full names should not be used. This shouldn't dissuade schools from using social media, though. Everything becomes much more straightforward once a policy has been established and all staff are aware of the rules.

It's generally better to use fewer platforms and be able to post to them more regularly, rather than splitting posts across many different places. This allows you to build up your following in key areas, and it means that parents know where to find what they're looking for. Based on demographics and ease of use, you might go for Facebook first and foremost, and Twitter and Instagram if you have time to maintain several platforms.

Many social media platforms are becoming increasingly money driven. Just because someone is following you doesn't mean that they will see what you post. Encourage your followers to click the 'see first' option on your page so that they're more likely to see your updates. If you've posted something really important or exciting you can also consider 'boosting' it with a small amount of money to help it reach more people – even £20 will help.

The idea of having a 'social media strategy' might sound daunting, but it doesn't have to be. Even writing a very basic outline of

(*continued*)

## Using social media positively (*continued*)

how you will use your social media platforms can give a really useful sense of direction. Consider the following:

- Why are you using social media?
- Who is your audience and what are they interested in?
- How can you best fit regular social media updates into your schedule?
- How can other members of staff support and enhance your use of social media?

Great school social media involves always having your finger on the pulse of school life and taking every opportunity to share it with your community. Set up a good line of communication between all teachers so that you know when shareable things are happening, and encourage staff to take photographs and videos themselves when you can't be there.

Some schools have central accounts for general school news, but every department also has their own account to share more specific content. This can be a great way of spreading the social media workload, and allows staff to show off their hard work, celebrate their students' achievements and communicate with parents.

Schools are all about the individuals that make them, so content that reflects this is always well received. Shout about individual student successes, share stories from the classroom and post things that allow parents to get to know the staff. Social media allows for a behind-the-scenes glimpse of school life that is really valuable to parents, so take advantage of having a community that genuinely cares about what you have to say.

### A tool for monitoring

The UK Safer Internet Centre has devised an app – based on similar ones widely used in the commercial world – which enables schools to monitor closely how they are talked about online, including when parents are posting critical comments.

Part of a toolkit called Boost, it crawls around the internet looking for posts, tweets and other mentions of the school's name and ranks the responses by sentiment – positive, negative or neutral – and influence by listing how many followers the person posting has or how many people the post is likely to reach through sharing.

For example, it would highlight something posted on the BBC news website as potentially high in influence, whereas a tweet lambasting a school for cancelling sports day from a parent with two followers would rank far lower.

Weekly or daily digests of the content are available, and it can also alert a school to particularly impactful negative posts. Schools can also hone the things that they search for; it's possible, for example, to search for a particular name.

It's a useful tool but how the school subsequently deals with the negative comment being brought to its attention is the more important part of the strategy, says David Wright, director of the UK Safer Internet Centre.

"If you spot something negative that a parent has said online, we advocate that schools reach out and say, 'we see you've posted this online [with the link]. We'd really welcome you to make a complaint, and here's a link to our complaints procedure.'"

"That not only demonstrates the posting might not be as private as they might have anticipated but also proves the school is active in that space, too. As a result, we find a lot of the time that those posts are removed."

https://boost.swgfl.org.uk/

## Use the law

Ultimately, and though schools may be reluctant to invoke it, they do have recourse to the law if a member of staff is being targeted in the media by a parent or anyone else: libel and defamation apply on Twitter and Facebook just as they do in print or broadcast. And while cyberbullying is not specifically defined as a crime, a perpetrator could be committing an offence under other laws including the Protection from Harassment Act (1997) under which it is an offence to send a communication that is indecent or grossly offensive or for the purpose of causing distress or anxiety to the recipient; or the Communications Act (2003), which covers sending via any electronic communication network a message or other matter that is deemed grossly offensive or of an indecent, obscene or menacing character. Fines or prison sentences of up to six months can be the penalty in both instances.

In extreme cases, parents have used the media as a tool for attacking a school which goes beyond an irate Facebook post into a darker realm.

One school, faced with intimidation over a months, was compelled to take out a harassment order against the parent as a last resort.

The parent, angered by the way the school had handled a complaint, launched a campaign of threats and intimidation, including threats to 'expose' the school in the press and bring in a documentary crew to highlight their wrongdoings. When the parent used the internet and social media to attack staff and governors at the school then the time had come to act.

Resorting to the law in such cases is not a step any governing body would take lightly. Not only does it cost in legal fees but it can absorb months of staff time, creating significant stress for those involved. Local authorities often advise against it and can be

(*continued*)

## Use the law (*continued*)

cautious about stirring things up but, as the head in this case says, sometimes resorting to the law is the only option when staff well-being and school reputation are under threat. "A good chat does work in many instances but the number of cases of schools being compelled down the legal route to tackle problems with parents that have got out of hand is on the increase. Fortunately, I had the backing of my governing body but it was still a hard decision."

## Case study: The TV experience

Vic Goddard shot to a sort of fame as head of the first school – Passmores Academy in Harlow, Essex – to feature in Channel 4's Educating . . . series of fly-on-the-wall documentaries in 2011.

In *Educating Essex*, the candid insights into pupil behaviour, teacher attitudes and the ups and downs of every-day-school life – captured in unforgiving detail by 65 cameras mounted in classrooms, corridors and offices – initially provoked some negative media coverage.

That swiftly abated, however, as uplifting stories about the students emerged and it became apparent just how passionately committed the staff were to the children.

When first approached by the TV company, Vic was attracted to the idea but didn't want to influence parents to say yes or no to the proposition, so all of the information was sent out by the producers.

> Parents trust the heads of their schools – research regularly points teachers up as the second most trusted profession after

(*continued*)

## Case study: The TV experience (*continued*)

> doctors – so I was very mindful of our influence on them and I didn't want parents to make decisions based on us.
>
> And, remember, we had no idea what the series was going to be like because we were the first.
>
> (Vic Goddard, Head, Passmores Academy, Harlow, July 2018)

There was a tactical reason for this, too. FoI had become a big issue for Passmores – as it has for many schools – and Vic wanted to avoid being subject to requests because of the work they entail. It proved a wise move.

> I did have a couple of really nasty FoIs afterwards with one reporter on a national broadsheet paper asking for any details I held on parents who refused to let their children be involved or any deleted scenes.
>
> But I was genuinely able to tell him I didn't hold any of that information. He then approached the production company and the case eventually went to the Information Commissioner's Office, but the request was turned down.
>
> He also wanted to know how much we got paid and he was particularly keen on how much I was receiving as the head. I was desperate to tell him that because it was laughable but the production company said it wasn't my information to share, which was quite frustrating!

Vic hadn't anticipated the level of interest that the series would generate and admits he and the school were probably a little naïve.

"I thought it would only be a small ripple in the media world; I had no idea we'd be in *The Sun* and *The Daily Mail*. The idea

(*continued*)

## Case study: The TV experience (*continued*)

was really just opening the doors to let parents see what we do on a normal day and try to treat it that way."

Once the programme was broadcast, some parents did comment in blogs and Facebook posts on some of the challenging behaviour seen on screen, but Vic and the staff took it all in their stride.

"Because I was very happy with the reality of how it portrayed being a teacher and having to deal with difficult teenagers sometimes, I never really felt that I had to justify myself to answer those questions. Nobody removed their child from the school because of the programme."

Was it good publicity, in the end? Passmores was oversubscribed before the programme was aired and remains so today.

"It may have influenced people whose child had some challenges at primary school, and maybe felt that the school hadn't done enough for them, so suddenly, we'd be high on their list of chosen schools. Part of me thinks that our intake became more challenging after that because parents could see the school gives a damn and would not give up on a child," says Vic.

On the other hand, he acknowledges, there may have been some parents who felt the school wasn't for them.

> We do Thursday morning tours for prospective parents and a group would come in, having seen the previous week's episode, and be surprised at how calm and orderly it was. Of course, on TV what you saw condensed into 47 minutes was a year's worth of activity so there was some surprise that it wasn't a madhouse!
>
> But you don't know how many parents didn't want to look round because it looked like a madhouse. You can never know. All I know is that we were full and we remain full.

(*continued*)

## Case study: The TV experience (*continued*)

Although he was happy with the way the production company dealt with the school and never felt traduced by editing, Vic found he was initially wrong-footed by other parts of the media, particularly the press and it is one area that he would approach differently were they to do another series (which has been offered and, as yet, declined).

> Whereas the broadcast media is so regimented and regulated, I found it much more difficult with the written press. And I think, with hindsight, I would talk to parents more about dealing with the door-stepping that went on and what their rights are around that and they don't need to engage.
>
> For example, in the very first episode, there was a young woman who had made an accusation that my deputy had pushed her. It took me a day to look at the CCTV, unpick it all, establish it wasn't true, call mum, and so on.
>
> When it went out, the press asked around our kids, found out where she lived, went round and got a couple of quotes out of her.
>
> I think the moment the press is involved, everybody's on the back foot. Everybody's reaction is, I've got to defend my family. That's utterly understandable but people have a right not to say anything, too, and skilled journalists are good at stopping people from doing that.
>
> But I would be more conscious of that now and I'd make it clear that parents should be free to call us if they need more support. As it happened, public opinion was very much on our side in that case, so we got less grief from the press generally after week 2.

(*continued*)

## Case study: The TV experience (*continued*)

There were other talking points; famously, an assistant principal bidding pupils goodbye with 'Clear off, scumbags,' and the shot of him jumping out from behind a door to surprise his deputy and flicking a V-sign at him.

These might have given an impression that the school had the air of, if not a 'madhouse,' then somewhere where the staff were very relaxed about their own behaviour.

Although they attracted mild condemnation from parts of the media initially, parents were not upset, he says. And once it became apparent that the show was popular, the media pendulum swung the other way.

"Parents loved the fact that we were human beings. I had many conversations with parents along the lines of 'that's why we like your school, because you do smile and enjoy each other's company.'"

"They loved our humanity."

JN

# Index

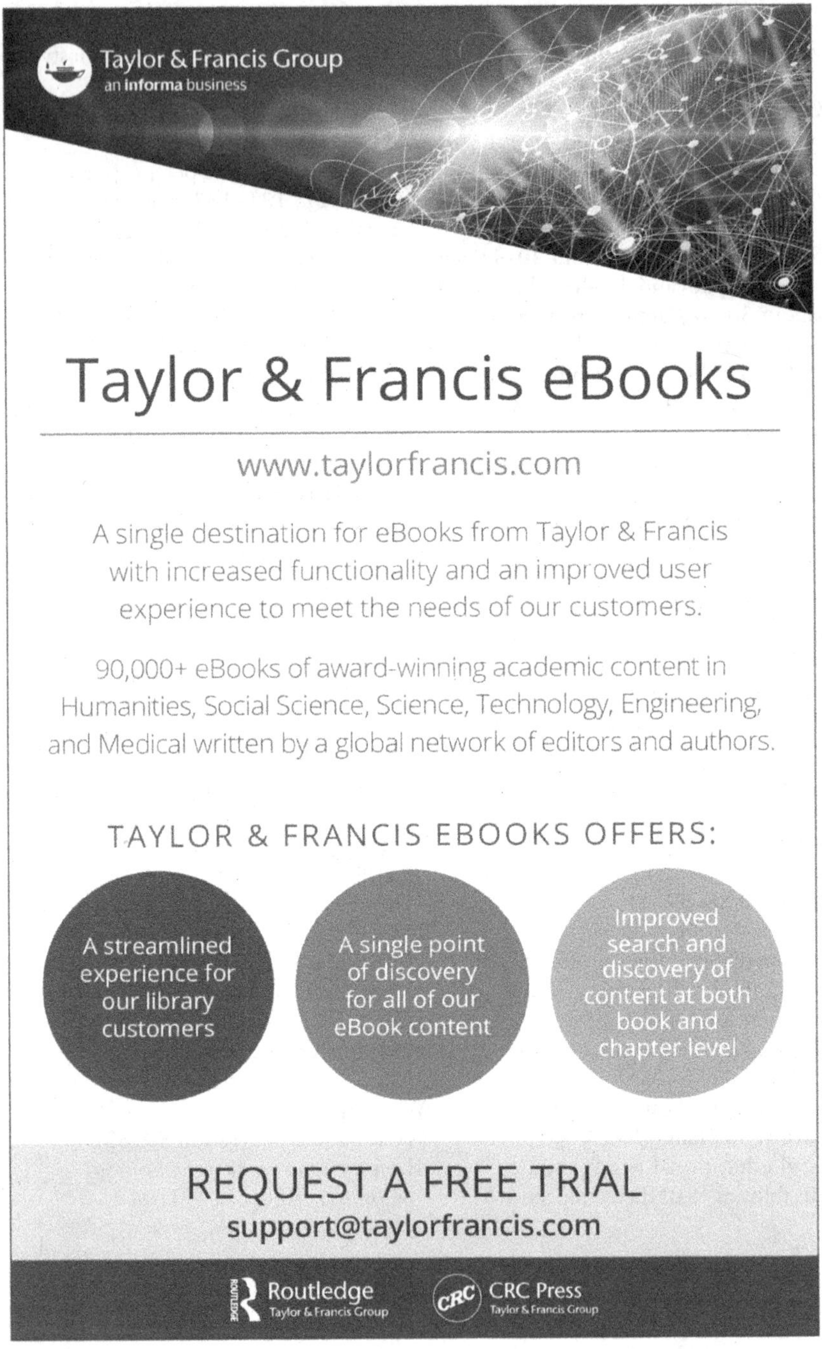